GOD'S GARDENERS

CREATION CARE STORIES FROM SINGAPORE AND MALAYSIA

Edited by Melissa Ong & Prarthini M. Selveindran

GRACEWORKS

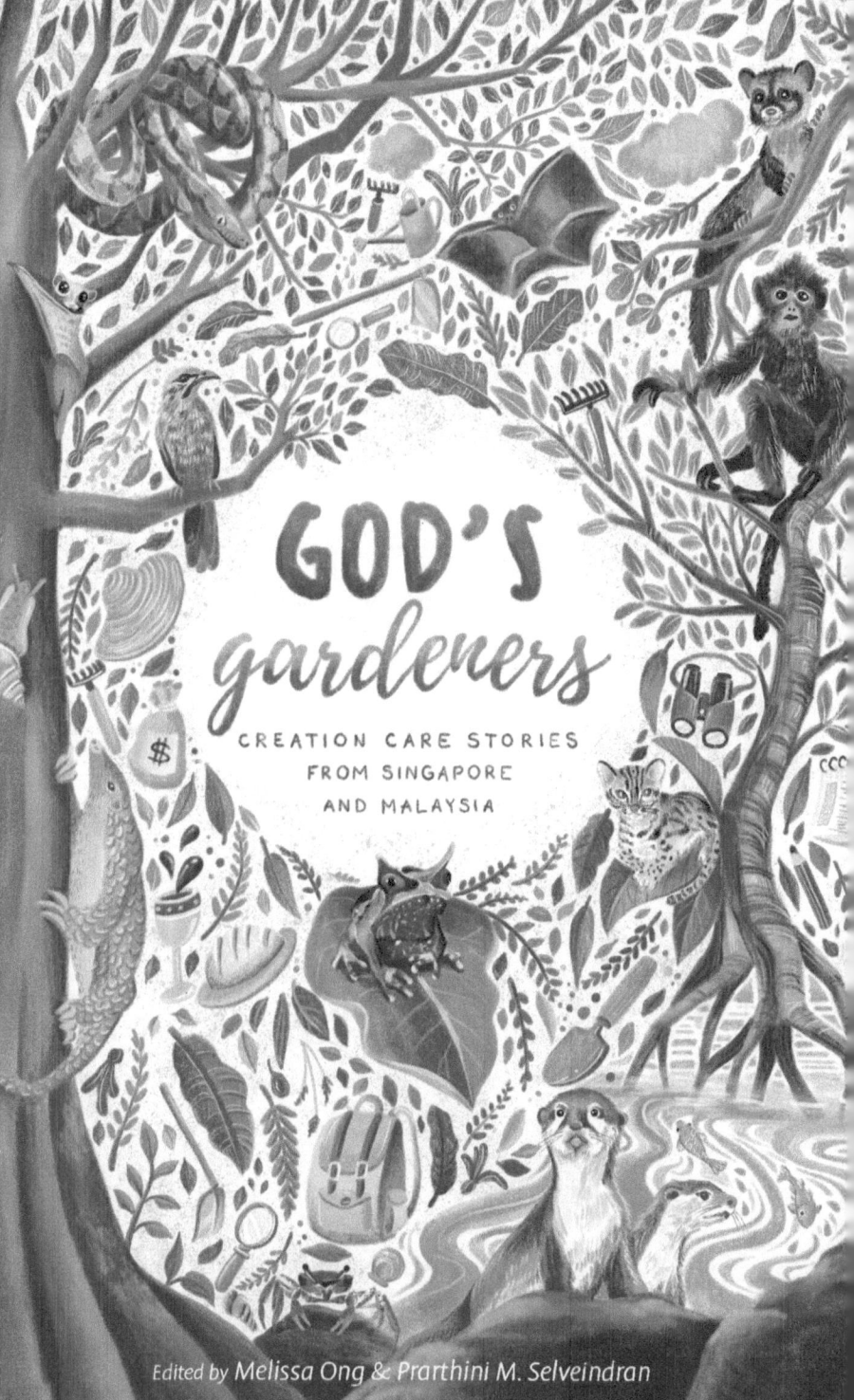

GOD'S GARDENERS: Creation Care Stories from Singapore and Malaysia
Copyright © 2020 by Graceworks Private Limited

The copyright for individual essays will reside with the individual authors.

All rights reserved. No part of this publication may be reproduced, stored in a retrieval system, or transmitted, in any form or by any means, electronic, mechanical, photocopying, recording or otherwise, without the prior written permission of the author, except in the case of brief quotations embodied in critical articles and reviews.

Published by Graceworks Private Limited
22 Sin Ming Lane, #04–76 Midview City, Singapore 573969
E-mail: enquiries@graceworks.com.sg
Website: www.graceworks.com.sg

All Scripture quotations, unless otherwise indicated, are taken from the Holy Bible, New International Version. Copyright © 1973, 1978, 1984 by International Bible Society. Used by permission of Zondervan. All rights reserved.

Scripture quotations marked "ESV" are taken from The Holy Bible, English Standard Version. Copyright © 2000; 2001 by Crossway Bibles, a division of Good News Publishers. Used by permission. All rights reserved.

Scripture quotations marked "KJV" are taken from the King James Version of the Bible.

Scripture quotations marked "MSG" are taken from The Message. Copyright © 1993, 1994, 1995, 1996, 2000, 2001, 2002. Used by permission of NavPress Publishing Group.

Scripture quotations marked "NRSV" are from the New Revised Standard Version Bible, copyright © 1989 the Division of Christian Education of the National Council of the Churches of Christ in the United States of America. Used by permission. All rights reserved.

Scripture quotations marked "NLT" are taken from the Holy Bible, New Living Translation, copyright © 1996, 2004, 2007 by Tyndale House Foundation. Used by permission of Tyndale House Publishers, Inc., Carol Stream, IL 60188. All rights reserved.

Scripture quotations marked "NASB" are taken from the New American Standard Bible® (NASB), Copyright © 1960, 1962, 1963, 1968, 1971, 1972, 1973, 1975, 1977, 1995 by The Lockman Foundation. Used by permission. www.Lockman.org

Cover design and illustrations by Elena Yeo
Typeface: Adobe Devanagari, Duper Pro

ISBN 978-981-14-3662-8

2 3 4 5 6 7 8 9 10 • 28 27 26 25 24 23 22 21 20

I had assumed that belief in a Creation implied that everything around us had divine origins and was thus guaranteed love, respect, and careful stewardship. The plight of our environment suggests otherwise. As the essays in this thought- and soul-provoking collection demonstrate, creation care is not automatic for everyone. And it won't happen without commitment and a re-examination of Scripture, our world, and our own faith. But my, how the benefits are manifold, tangible, and within reach!

Shawn Lum
President, Nature Society (Singapore)

Read this book if you care for God's creation! Written from the perspective of people with deep roots in the "Little Red Dot" and Malaysia, these stories and reflections demonstrate the personal, theological, and biblical underpinnings of the contributors. A privatised faith? Absolutely not! The ecological crisis cannot be avoided or ignored, but must be addressed by the individual and the Church, whose missional quest in caring for creation is gaining momentum. This book provides some thoughts and actions for us all. "The earth is the Lord's and all that is in it, the world, and those who live in it!" (Psalm 24:1 NRSV).

Tan Yak-hwee
Associate Professor, Tainan Theological College, Taiwan
Katong Presbyterian Church, Singapore

If you have been looking for everyday stewards of the earth, you can find them and their stories in this inspiring collection. They are people from different walks of life who care about our environment and take action through their work and in their daily practices. They walk the talk, and are united by a strong common faith. Their stories are worth reading and sharing.

Tan Beng Chiak
Educator

To bear fruit requires courage. This book encourages the Church, while demonstrating the courage of Christians in tending to a Creation that is groaning for Christ who is reconciling and making the whole cosmos new.

Inspiring, provocative and practical are the stories, reflections and interludes. The nurturing care of the stewards and contributors of this book project is evident in the pages and have borne fruit. I commend this refreshing work to the Singapore Church in hope that she will live out her mandate as *God's Gardeners* and bear fruit—abundant fruit over all the earth to the glory of God as the waters cover the seas.

Ronald JJ Wong
National Coordinator of Micah Singapore
Author, The Justice Demand: Social Justice & the Singapore Church

This book is a sign of hope. Christians and churches all over the world are stepping up to love the people and places where God has planted them, and Singapore is no exception. My love for God's creation was first kindled while growing up in this city, so I am greatly encouraged. Inspiring, practical, and biblically grounded, this book features rich stories and wisdom from a diverse cast of creation care leaders and practitioners. Read *God's Gardeners* and be empowered to join in the good work that God calls all of us to do.

Ben Lowe
Chair, A Rocha USA
Chair, Evangelicals for Social Action

One of Creation's most distinctive features is that it is full of diversity and unexpected surprises. *God's Gardeners* is like a microcosm of Creation. Just when you think that this book is about the theology of Creation, you then discover that it's also about giant fruit bats being durian pollinators. Then as you're getting your head around that, you are challenged to be salt and light by modelling living within the ecological carrying capacity of the earth. Next, you're into a church building project—but with a difference. And so on... *God's Gardeners* takes you through a challenging but hopeful and surprising journey—truly an original and inspiring book!

Simon Stuart
Director of Strategic Conservation, Synchronicity Earth
A Rocha International Trustee

For Miranda

Contents

Foreword xiii
Peter Harris

Acknowledgements xv

Preface xix
The Editors

**The Ecology of Salvation and the Salvation of Ecology
—*Theological Overview*** xxv
Andrew Peh

1. **Missional Creation Care** 5
   David Gould

2. **Building a Building and a People** 13
   Goh Wei Leong & Lam Kuo Yung

3. **Paying Attention in the Anthropocene** 21
   Mary-Ruth Low

BEAUTY

4. Amphibian Diversity in Urban Parks: Attending to Creation in the City 33
   Melissa Ong & Prarthini M. Selveindran

5. Nurturing Wonder-filled Children 41
   Shai Kroeker

6. Community is a Lot Like a Garden 51
   Priscilla Teh

DOMINION

7. Finances, Social Justice & Climate Action: A Paradoxical Approach 61
   Eunice Ng

8. Thinking Christianly about Food 73
   Reuben Ang

9. God Unchanging in a Changing Climate 81
   Hoi Wen Au Yong

10. Event Stewardship 89
    Shoni Duesling

11. Sayang Kalimantan   99
Wally Tham

12. Only One Earth   105
Khee Shihui

13. Trusting in the Gardener's Pruning   117
Shirene Chen & Ken Yeong

Afterword   125
Quek Tze-Ming

Appendix   131

Foreword

Peter Harris

Many people who love nature think of exotic species when they envisage rarities—but here is a true rarity—a book about the care of creation that is rooted in Singaporean and Malaysian sensibilities. It is essential that we in the West listen and learn from the experience and reflections of Christians in this part of the world because they have felt the great crisis of the loss of life on earth as directly as anyone else on the planet.

If we are to truly understand the magnitude of challenges that are global in scale, we must begin with careful listening to the voices of different people who, in their own places, in their own particular times, and in true community with all that they come to know right there of God's glorious creation, have been prepared to love the places where they live. After all, "[God] marked out their appointed times in history and the boundaries of their lands. God did this so that they would seek him and perhaps reach out for him and find him, though he is not far from any one of us." (Acts 17: 26–27)

"Love is never abstract," wrote Wendell Berry. "It does not adhere to the universe or the planet or the nation or the institution or the profession, but to the singular sparrows of the street, the lilies of the field, 'the least of these my brethren.'"[1] The authors of this book are under no illusion of what true love for nature may mean. Rather than looking towards a sunset glow of short-lived feelings about how beautiful everything is, or how individual heroism might "make a difference", we find in this book a more authentic pattern of the self-giving, sacrificial passion of Jesus. The authors invite us to follow in that way, which leads us to a deeper wisdom, even if it takes us on harder roads. I know from my own time in cities and in the field with them that they have indeed been compelled by the love that Berry writes about.

The double challenge offered here is to recover a sense of what true value is within a genuinely flourishing economy and ecology, and to rediscover a biblical theology that does justice to the whole of creation, not merely human well-being. With these authors, we are in good hands.

---

[1] Wendell Berry, *What Are People For* (San Francisco, CA: North Point, 1990), 200.

Acknowledgements

We are deeply indebted to all our writer-contributors who generously shared their stories in this book. Without your time, effort and thought, this book could not have come into being, and for that we express our sincere gratitude. We are also thankful for Elena who illustrated our book; your artistry and partnership are such gifts to us.

I (Mel) am immensely grateful to Zion Bishan BP Church for supporting both my work and that of A Rocha since 2005, and embracing creation care as mission. Thank you for supporting me financially in the writing of this book.

I (Prarthi) would like to thank FES for recognising and affirming the value of this work—not just for our students, but for the Singapore Church at large. Thank you for allowing me a measure of flexibility in my schedule to expend time and energy into this project.

For our various friends, supporters and loved ones who have journeyed alongside us throughout this endeavour,

our hearts are filled with gratitude for your love, support and kindness:

I (Prarthi) am especially grateful to my fiancé, Isaac, who spent considerable time and effort in editing some of the stories and helping us put together our chapter. I (Mel) am so blessed to have the support of Dan my husband, and my parents who have always believed in me and encouraged me. Thank you. To Kevin Behan, my mentor and teacher: I am forever grateful for your wisdom and friendship.

We have a huge appreciation for Graceworks. Thank you for entrusting us with this idea and granting us the freedom to nurture and grow it into a full-fledged book. Through the process of envisioning this book, as well as curating and editing the stories that our friends lived, both of us have grown tremendously.

This book would not have been possible without Peter and Miranda Harris and the existence of A Rocha. Both Peter and Miranda have a deep love and concern for Singapore and Malaysia and our blossoming local creation care movement. Their lives give us courage and strength, and they have modelled for us a joyful and redemptive way of *being* in creation and in community. We are inspired by their beautiful witness of caring for God's earth in hope, faith and love. I (Mel) owe much of who I am to them because of their love, mentorship and friendship. A Rocha saved me in many ways and I am eternally grateful to Peter and Miranda for showing me that the creation God loves is worth fighting for. We are also deeply thankful to Chris Naylor, A

Rocha International's Executive Director, for his support to Melissa and Friends of A Rocha in Singapore and for cheering us on in this project. (*At the time of writing, Peter, Miranda, Chris and his wife Susanna were involved in a horrific car accident in Port Elizabeth, South Africa. Miranda, Chris and Susanna did not survive. We grieve alongside their families and the global creation care community.*)

Throughout this journey, both of us had moments of self-doubt as we were daunted by the task ahead of us. We were driven to pray and commit this labour of love into God's hands. We give thanks for his faithfulness towards us. May he use this book for his good purpose.

Preface

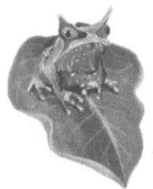

2019 poised to be really hot year[1]
Mass extinction is hard to stomach[2]
Climate Change and the New Age of Extinction[3]
Take Action Now: Declare a Climate Emergency[4]

This kind of news has become the new normal. We read of the recent Global Climate Strike, where millions of youth worldwide rallied in protesting the climate crisis. We hear the impassioned, "How dare you!" speech by Swedish schoolgirl Greta Thunberg, which has been integral in

---

1 Ai-Lien Chang, "2019 poised to be really hot year," *Straits Times*, March 22, 2019, https://www.straitstimes.com/singapore/environment/2019-poised-to-be-really-hot-year.

2 "Mass extinction is hard to stomach," *Straits Times*, May 12, 2019, https://www.straitstimes.com/opinion/mass-extinction-is-hard-to-stomach.

3 Elizabeth Kolbert, "Climate Change and the New Age of Extinction," *New Yorker*, May 13, 2019, https://www.newyorker.com/magazine/2019/05/20/climate-change-and-the-new-age-of-extinction.

4 NationAction, "Take Action Now: Declare a Climate Emergency," *Nation*, Oct. 30, 2019, https://www.thenation.com/article/take-action-now-declare-a-climate-emergency/.

this youth climate change movement, at the United Nations (UN) Climate Action Summit where she rebuked world leaders for their inadequate response to climate concerns.[5] Much of the climate movement today is characterised by a blame-and-shame posture, fury, guilt, eco-anxiety, and hopelessness.

We simply can't ignore the reality that our planet is in severe crisis. As Christians, how can we live within these realities? How do we respond to these messages of despair and anger that barrage us?

At the end of 2018, we were approached by Graceworks to consider writing a book on caring for creation that was contextualised to Singapore. We were at first apprehensive—there are so many well-written books on creation care. Was another one really necessary?

In the years that we've advocated for 'creation care', we have come to know kindred spirits doing good work where they are in embodying God's love for creation. Many of them have become dear friends, and their faithfulness fills these pages. Their stories speak of their care for creation as love in action, as worship, as stewardship, discipleship, mission, justice, joyful living, and ultimately as a way of *being* in God's world. Their lives reflect a holistic understanding of the gospel: declaring the Lordship of Christ cannot be separated from caring for his creation.

---

5 Tessa Oh, "Explainer: Who is Greta Thunberg and how have grown-ups taken to this teenage climate activist," *Today Singapore*, Sept. 27, 2019, https://www.todayonline.com/singapore/explainer-who-greta-thunberg-and-how-have-grown-ups-taken-teenage-climate-activist.

We learnt this best from Peter and Miranda Harris, who had the courageous vision to establish a bird observatory in southern Portugal in 1983 that grew into A Rocha, an international network of organisations working in 21 countries committed to engaging communities in nature conservation. We are grateful for their pioneering work of Christians in conservation and the global creation care movement, for their costly commitment to community and embrace of indigenous expressions of creation care. They have lived these out through faith, hope and love. Both Peter and Miranda have visited Singapore and Malaysia numerous times, sharing their wisdom and heart for God's world through various seminars, talks, and conversations over meals. Their stories of hope from the A Rocha family—how Christians were involved in restoring habitats and transforming communities out of love for God—have inspired many and served as a catalyst to the local movement here. They nurtured deep relationships with many in both Singapore and Malaysia and longed to see creation care flourish here.

There certainly isn't a fixed way to "do" creation care, and we wanted to reflect that diversity and breadth of expression in this book. So what you have before you is a *rojak* of personal testimonies (profiles), commentary pieces on macro issues, and several case studies. Marking each segment are interludes for contemplation— *Ecology*, *Beauty*, *Dominion*, *Shalom*, and *St Francis*—which speak into the chapters that follow. Finally, as theology shapes our understanding of ecology and anthropology, the bookends offer biblical grounding.

This book is not about saving the planet. We can't. Neither is it meant to prescribe a way of living nor dictate 10 easy steps on how to fix the climate. We've called our book, *God's Gardeners* and borrow from the wise words of Peter Harris to express the heart of this metaphor: "...gardening reminds us that God is the one giving the growth, and not us. Gardening, even in a groaning creation, is good hard work, restful for the soul and body. And it is work in which we see both frustration and fruit. Even so, while we are gardening the earth we cooperate with our loving Creator God who alone gives all the conditions under which we can 'produce' anything. Whatever we call our work—gardening, earth-keeping, nature conservation—we need to pray that we will be faithful and grateful in blessing creation and not be fretful or restless in our creatureliness."[6]

For many Singaporeans, the word 'garden' may conjure manicured green spaces for human recreation. Yet God's garden is marvellously wild and wondrous in all its diversity and we hope this book offers a glimpse of what tending and blessing our patch of creation looks like with a local *flavah*! These are stories of humble acts performed with love that we desire to share with the Church. We hope they inspire you and encourage those of you who feel alone in your creation care journey.

These actions may seem meagre in the face of mass extinctions and climate calamities, yet we believe and know that love never fails. Our hope lies in the One who is renewing

---

6 Peter Harris, "Loving where we are," *A Rocha Planetwise Blog*, Jan. 15, 2016, https://blog.arocha.org/en/loving-where-we-are/.

and reconciling all creation to himself. As we pray, "Thy Kingdom come on Earth as it is in Heaven", we believe that in him our labour is not in vain.

"Be joyful though you have considered all the facts... Practice resurrection."[7] ~Wendell Berry

Love,
Mel & Prarthi
November 2019

---

7 Wendell Berry, "Manifesto: The Mad Farmer Liberation Front" from *The Country of Marriage* (New York City, NY: Harcourt Brace Jovanovich, 1973).

THE ECOLOGY OF SALVATION AND THE SALVATION OF ECOLOGY

—*THEOLOGICAL OVERVIEW*—

Andrew Peh

Rev Dr Andrew Peh, PhD (Asbury Theological Seminary) is a faculty of Trinity Theological College and lectures in the area of missions and mission history. His interests are in the history of Christianity in Asia and mission trends in the 21st century, which includes, not least of all, creation care as part of God's mission in our world. His favourite animal is the polar bear and he hopes that it will continue to thrive as 'the king' of the arctic.

It was not too long ago that my interest in ecology and its intersection with Christianity was piqued, especially in light of the Indonesian forest fires that severely impacted Singapore. It grew as I was inundated daily with news of calamities such as droughts, floods, heatwaves, earthquakes, hurricanes and typhoons, the frequency and intensity of which were increasing. Concurrently, news of global warming and Earth's sixth mass extinction due to human-driven causes such as habitat destruction and our insatiable demand for 'black gold', metals and minerals, spurred my desire to make sense of these alarming developments from a biblical perspective.

A more robust theology of ecology is seemingly lacking within the Singapore Church (perhaps I have not been sufficiently industrious in my search) and there seems to be a disconcerting reticence among our Christian academics and pastors in the area of stewardship/creation care. This has been further exacerbated by a consumerist culture that is apathetic to the groans of creation. It may also be that the current environmental crisis is in part the result of the Church's defective hermeneutic, where we have misunderstood and misrepresented God's intention in giving humanity the "exercise of dominion" (or to subdue) as recorded in the creation account.

God's plan and act of salvation as spelled out in Scripture involves the redemption of all creation and is what Luke records in Acts 3:21 (NLT) as the "restoration of all things". We read in Ephesians 1:10 that God has a plan (*oikonomia*) for the fullness of time to bring everything in heaven and earth together in reconciliation under the headship of Jesus Christ—all things, things in heaven and things on earth; things visible and invisible (Colossians 1:15–20). Howard Snyder underscores the fact that "God's plan of redemption is as broad as the scope of creation and the depth of sin, for 'where sin abounded, grace (has) much more (abounded)' (Romans 5:20 KJV)."[1]

It is interesting to me, then, that we have often erroneously reduced and capitalised on God's salvation to feature humanity as the primary and possibly singular focus of God's salvific plan. But the biblical data is such that all things, all creation, will be redeemed and renewed so that we can speak of a new heaven and a new earth. God's mission is wider and more expansive than the redemption of humanity!

In *The Mission of God*, Christopher Wright wrote that by reminding readers of the biblical value of the rest of creation he is by no means simply *equating* human value with the non-human creatures, nor is he in any way reducing the crucial theological importance of the doctrine of humanity, the image of God, and the person-redeeming work of the cross. He noted that Jesus managed both to *affirm* the value of every sparrow to God the Father while simultaneously confirming that humans are of greater value. In emphasising an inclusion for creation in God's redemption plan, Wright asserts:

---

[1] Howard Snyder, "Salvation Means Creation Healed: Creation, Cross, Kingdom and Mission," *Asbury Journal*, Vol. 62, no.1 (2007): 9–47, https://place.asburyseminary.edu/cgi/viewcontent.cgi?article=1088&context=asburyjournal.

> All I am trying to do is to encourage evangelicals to read their whole Bibles, and to see the great arc that spans from Genesis 1–2 to Revelation 21–22, and to take Eph. 1:9–10, and Col. 1:15–20 with full seriousness—for there it is clear that Paul sees personal redemption within a staggeringly cosmic and universal framework.[2]

Wright is right that if we were to adopt a principally anthropocentric perspective of salvation and redemption, we would be, in effect, excising Genesis 1–2 and Revelation 21–22 from our Bibles, since it is in Genesis 3 that we read of the accounts for the fall of humanity, and Revelation 20 concludes with the binding and the final judgement of Satan. Genesis 1 and 2 recount God's affirmation of his creation—he proclaims that it was good at the end of each day. Then following the creation of land creatures and Adam and Eve on the sixth day, he declares that all he had made was very good! Yet the fall of mankind in Genesis 3 was to affect the whole of the created order. Human sin and evil have permeated the natural order as well as the human and spiritual reality. Therefore creation is also in need of redemption, for which Revelation 21 not only speaks of a new heaven, but a new earth as well! As Wright eloquently sums up:

> Creation shares in the effect of humanity's sin but we human beings get to share in the fullness of creation's redemption. And that is the right way round to put it.

---

2 Ed Stetzer, "Monday is for Missiology: Christopher Wright on Christian Mission," *Christianity Today*, Jan. 23, 2012, https://www.christianitytoday.com/edstetzer/2012/january/monday-is-for-missiology-christopher-wright-on-christian.html.

We get saved along with creation; and not that we get saved out of creation. God's intention is to redeem that whole of creation and we can be a part of that and in so doing become a part of the new creation.[3]

The point that Wright and Snyder (and other like-minded scholars) are making is that we cannot afford to be myopic or insular in our theological understanding of salvation and redemption, focusing exclusively on humanity as the crown of creation and omitting all non-human creation. As we become attentive to Scripture, we will begin to have a more holistic perspective of God's salvation, which includes but is not limited to humanity.

The ecology of human sin, the consequences on creation and the efficacy of God's redemption are all intricately and intimately tied up to the atoning work of Jesus Christ. Essentially it is getting the ecology of salvation right that makes for a more robust effort at the salvation of our ecology. Hence, as we survey the biblical data as well as various theological articulations in more recent years (including Sandra Richter's *A Biblical Theology of Creation Care*[4] and Pope Francis' *Laudato Si*),[5] Snyder's clarion call is that, as Christians, we

---

3 Christopher Wright, "Creation, Gospel and Mission," *OMF*, March 14, 2019, https://omf.org/blog/2019/03/14/creation-gospel-and-mission/. See also Chris Wright, "Creation Care," Oct. 23, 2013, John Stott London Lecture 2013, MPEG-4, 45:45, https://www.youtube.com/watch?v=wvsqrFizQ7k.

4 Sandra Richter, "A Biblical Theology of Creation Care", *Asbury Journal*: Vol. 62, no. 1 (2007): 67–76, https://place.asburyseminary.edu/cgi/viewcontent.cgi?article=1090&context=asburyjournal.

5 "Encyclical Letter Laudato Si' of the Holy Father Francis on Care for Our Common Home," *Vatican*, accessed Nov. 14, 2019, http://w2.vat-

...need to think clearly about God's creation — both its goodness and its groaning; both as God's gift and as the environment within which God is reconciling "to Himself all things, whether on earth or in heaven, by making peace through the blood of (the) cross" (Colossians 1:2). This is a matter of theology, of discipleship, and of Christian mission.[6]

Most of us are familiar with the story of Jonah, which is a story often repeated at Sunday school classes. As I reread the story of this reluctant prophet, there are hints that God's redemptive plans are more comprehensive than Jonah ever perceived.

It is a story that invites us to wonder at the magnanimity of God's compassion for the Ninevites, his prodigal love for Jonah and radical inclusion of creation in his salvation plan—a big fish served as his instrument for bringing Jonah to submission; the king of Nineveh ensured that even the animals in his kingdom were included in a fast of repentance that resulted in God's gracious forgiveness of the whole of Nineveh; God's provision of a plant and a worm as a lesson to remind Jonah that He is a God who is intimately concerned with all that He has created.

In *God in Pursuit*, Bishop Emeritus Robert Solomon wrote:

> Jonah was an unlikely prophet. His heart was not fully in God's work, he had his own issues with sin, and

---

ican.va/content/francesco/en/encyclicals/documents/papa-francesco_20150524_enciclica-laudato-si.html.

6 Snyder, "Salvation Means".

he held a wrong understanding of God and His ways. He was at first an unwilling instrument in God's hands, then a willing but prejudiced one. Are we like Jonah? Are we trying to flee God? Or are we doing His work out of duty, without reflecting His character? Are we harbouring prejudices that are incongruent with being a child of God and a servant of Christ?[7]

The story of Jonah (especially Jonah 4) highlights the plight of an unlikely prophet of God and God's loving pursuit of this reluctant and obstinate prophet. Perhaps in regard to caring for creation, we are similarly unconvinced, uninterested and even unwilling. But God's question to Jonah is equally valid for us: "If you feel compassionate about the destruction of a vine you did not create, shouldn't I be concerned about the destruction of people and animals I did create?"

While I agree that the biblical accounts pay special attention to human salvation, we are nonetheless cognisant that God's salvation includes and involves His entire creation. David Bosch is on point when he wrote: "The time is long past that we can afford to exclude the environment from our missionary agenda."[8]

For if God is concerned about creation, should we not also be similarly concerned?

---

[7] Robert Solomon, *God in Pursuit: Lessons from the Book of Jonah* (Singapore: Bible Society of Singapore, 2017), 129.

[8] David Bosch, *Believing in the Future: Towards a Missiology of Western Culture* (Valley Forge, PE: Trinity Press International, 1995), 55.

The word *ecology* refers to the relationship of living things to their environment and to each other. Based on the Greek word *oikos* for "household", it was first coined by German zoologist Ernst Haeckel in 1866. Everything has its proper place, functioning and intrinsic value in God's "household"; the earth is the Lord's (Psalm 24:1). It is a rich term that helps us understand the diversity, complexity and interconnectedness of all of life, which is lovingly sustained by God (Psalm 104).

When applied to the Christian doctrine of sin, the extent of the effects of sin is not merely located in the vertical axis between God and humanity, but is also evident in the horizontal ramifications affecting human relationships as well as hurting the rest of creation (both animate and inanimate). In other words, sin injures not only our relationship with God, but also with ourselves, with other people, and with the non-human creation. Howard Snyder refers to this as the "ecology of sin". He contends that God's redemptive plan is fundamentally *ecological*, where "everything, absolutely everything, above and below, visible and invisible … everything got started in him and finds its purpose in him" (Colossians 1:16 MSG). Ecology shows us the intricacy and interdependence of all the parts, and gives us a better appreciation of the mission of God, which involves humanity and includes all of God's creation.

MISSIONAL CREATION CARE

David Gould

David's interest in creation care started with a desire to make the buildings he was designing more sustainable in their use of materials and energy. While travelling in East Asia he was deeply saddened by the environmental devastation that he saw, much of it driven by the insatiable demands of the global economy. As he thought and prayed about this he came to realise that creation care is an integral part of God's mission for his people; that the gospel of Christ is good news not just for individuals but for the whole of creation; and that we should do all we can to proclaim and live out this good news. Since 2012 he has been tasked by Overseas Missionary Fellowship (OMF) International to explore the growing ecological crisis, its impacts on the peoples of East Asia, and appropriate missional responses.

Creation Care in the Mission of OMF International

In OMF we define creation care as "the responsible stewardship by humankind of the earth and its life forms, for the Lord's sake." We believe that "The earth is the LORD's, and everything in it" (Psalm 24:1); that we are called to work the earth and take care of it (Genesis 2:15); and that we cannot truly love our neighbours without caring for the land and ecosystems on which they (and we) depend. We need to care for both people and places.

Since the 1950s, OMF's pioneering work among the tribal peoples of the Philippines and Thailand has integrated evangelism with teaching sustainable agriculture. In his 1982 book *Keeping Body and Soul Together*, Denis Lane described the integration of spiritual and farming instruction in north Thailand:

> Because the Gospel had removed the binding fear of the spirits, one *Pwo Karen* Christian dared to plant a field regarded by his unbelieving neighbours as spirit-haunted. They would not dare to touch it, but he reaped a rich harvest that year. Yet there was no separation between the spiritual and the practical. The missionaries stood with this man in a prayer battle against what he and they knew to be real spiritual forces. One missionary prayed and taught the spiritual warfare, and another worked and taught soils and seeds, and both contributed to a harvest where before there was nothing but weeds.

Now we are facing unprecedented ecological challenges that necessitate a fresh exploration of how we should include creation care ministry in our missionary work. So OMF has prepared a statement of the "Theological Basis for Creation Care".[1]

And we have formulated three aspirations for our ministry:

- *As part of being disciples we should practise creation care:* We recognise that our actions should be consistent with our words. We want to be good stewards of all the resources entrusted to us.

- *As part of our disciple-making we should teach creation care*: Creation care is included in our orientation courses for those joining OMF, and in our e-Learning programmes. We explore creation care themes with churches, theological seminaries, other mission agencies, and in student ministry.

- *As part of mission strategy we should consider creation care*: One of OMF's core values is to lead from the ministry context, and the need for creation care ministry varies widely. In addition to ministry in rural communities, there are new opportunities in the cities of East Asia. There is the ever-present challenge of balancing the ministry of word and deed. On the one hand, if we seek to address ecological challenges simply as a basis for evangelism, our work will lack effectiveness and conviction, and we will not win a hearing for the gospel. On the other hand, if we focus solely on addressing these challenges, we will miss opportunities for evangelism in our mission.

---

[1] See https://omf.org/wp-content/uploads/2016/04/MRT-9.1-May-2014-Missional-Creation-Care.pdf?x86309.

Three Examples of Missional Creation Care in Practice
*Note: names have been changed

Mongolia: Akhai* had seen his three brothers die as a result of alcohol addiction. One day, his girlfriend Ulzi* persuaded him to go to church with her. There he heard the gospel and received new life in Christ. He no longer needed to drink alcohol. Akhai and Ulzi were married and now serve those who wrestle with alcohol addiction, offering them hope founded on Christ.

The Lord called Paul* to work with Akhai and Ulzi. Paul is a specialist in waste management who has a heart for mission. During his visits, Paul saw the potential to 'upcycle' waste paper to provide fuel bricks for sale. He then trained Akhai's and Ulzi's team to make and use the tools needed to process the waste. The 'fuel from waste' project provides a cleaner alternative to burning coal, which produces hazardous smoke. By offering his skills, Paul has given Akhai's and Ulzi's ministry the opportunity to grow, and they are now able to start similar work in other cities. Akhai is a gifted evangelist and leader, and as a result of this partnership, more people are coming to faith in Christ, and churches are being planted.

Manila: Across the global south and east, migration to the cities in response to ecological and other challenges presents unprecedented opportunities for mission. Kamal* reluctantly brought his family to live in Manila because he did not want his children "to grow up with guns". In his community in the city, many are suffering from malnutrition. As one of the leaders of the community, he welcomes the friendship of those who are offering training in providing good nutrition for children.

Bangkok: People of different faiths are meeting to discuss ways of improving the health and welfare of the urban poor. Promoting the use of simple water filters can be very effective, as it provides employment opportunities, affordable and potable water, as well as opportunities to introduce people to the "living water" of Christ.

A Challenge for the Churches of Singapore

In this time of ecological crisis, what does it mean for churches to be in the world, but not of it? How can they embody the Kingdom of God, instead of succumbing to the excessive consumerism that characterises much of the global economy? If churches are to be true salt and light in society, they must rise to the challenge of modelling life that thrives within the ecological carrying capacity of the earth. I believe that the stories that follow in this book will provide many valuable insights into what this can look like.

The skills and experience needed to respond to this challenge are significant in cross-cultural mission. The possibilities are endless: they include environmental conservation and consultancy; sustainable eco-tourism; waste management; and training local people in alternative energy technology, efficient food production, and water purification. All such activities can demonstrate the love of Christ in practical ways, and foster friendships in which the gospel can be shared. The churches in Singapore, in partnership with seminaries and mission agencies, are well placed to mobilise, equip, commission, and support those with the necessary skills and experience, who are called to participate in creation care integral mission.

To start with, churches can initiate "vision trips" to help scope the work that is needed, and to help discern God's calling to this kind of work. Some may then make occasional short visits to work with local believers and specialists to develop appropriate responses and training. Others may be called and sent out to work long-term with universities and other agencies, or to develop missional businesses.

It is important that those who are sent out are prepared to give an account of the hope that they have in Christ. By testifying to this hope, they can inspire the locals on the field to care for their land and its peoples. After all, the gospel is good news not just for people, but for all creation. Those who are sent out will need servant hearts, with real compassion for the people they are called to serve. And they should be willing to learn and adapt to local conditions, rather than going with ready-made solutions to perceived problems.

Finally, they need to be willing to share what they have learned when they return home. As others in the church hear about their experiences on the field, they too will be inspired to renew their commitment to creation care. Some may be encouraged to do their own outreach, while others continue to mobilise, support and pray for this kind of ministry. The "returnees" can also encourage their church to "welcome the stranger"—those who come to Singapore with stories and insights to share from other lands. Some of them can become very effective mobilisers for mission in their home countries, and perhaps be sent out in their turn.

Walking in step with the biblical mandate for creation care is an intrinsic part of God's purposes for all people, rather than just being an optional extra for "green Christians". It connects people and places, and shows a deep concern for the flourishing of all life. It follows that we should embrace creation care as part of our sharing and demonstration of the gospel of Christ.

BUILDING A BUILDING AND A PEOPLE

Goh Wei Leong & Lam Kuo Yung

Dr Goh Wei Leong co-founded and chairs HealthServe, an NGO that reaches out to under-served foreign workers in Singapore. HealthServe and Wei Leong were awarded the Singaporean of the Year 2017. He is a member of the global board of Operation Mobilisation International and chairs OM's Mercy Teams International. An elder of his church, Katong Presbyterian, Wei Leong is also passionate about social justice and connecting people to one another. Wei Leong keeps a regular rhythm of rest, reflection and work to constantly calibrate true north.

Rev Lam Kuo Yung, senior pastor of Katong Presbyterian Church, is married to Lois Kwan and they have three children. They are homeschooling their children and are grateful for the benefits that it avails. In his free time, he enjoys cycling, fishing and camping. Kuo Yung is also author of the book Together Alive: Rediscovering the Lost Art of Living Together.

Creation care has always been one of Katong Presbyterian Church's (KPC) five core values. As we embarked on our church building project, we wanted the process and the final building to be an expression of good stewardship of the earth's resources. Moreover, we hoped that our church community would catch our passion and practice creation care not only in church, but also in their day-to-day life. This is our story about how KPC grew together to become better caretakers of the earth, and the beautiful work of changing a culture in community.

Building His Church

Our church renovation project started out of a practical need. Due to its age, parts of the church building were falling into disrepair. We gathered suggestions about design ideas and plans for the new building from our members. Their feedback made us realise that we could do so much more than merely operating in a "business as usual" manner—that is, by simply adding a few rooms, increasing the size of space for greater ease of usage, and continuing customary church practice. Rather, this church building project was a great opportunity to live out our core values and build up our community as well.

Hence, we intentionally integrated discipleship and servanthood into this process. As we involved the whole church in thinking about and working on this project, we grew to embody the missional values of the church:

1. Lovers of all people
2. Disciples making disciples

3. Bridge builders across generations
4. Upholders of justice and mercy
5. Caretakers of the earth

For KPC, creation care is an integral part of good discipleship, that is, an expression of how we love God and our neighbour. Once we recognise that God has created all things, we demonstrate our worship of him by looking after the earth he has entrusted to us. In doing so, we will also end up caring for his people. Our neighbours who have limited access to resources are often the most vulnerable to environmental threats and most adversely affected by its degradation. It is not too far a stretch to see that taking good care of creation is an extension of upholding justice and mercy for our neighbours in these regions.

A Collective Endeavour

We called our renovation project, "The Community Building Project". It was an intentionally ambiguous title to reflect our purposes of building both the physical church and the church community. This journey took eight years! But our church community enjoyed and grew so much through the process that toward the end, completing the physical building became the secondary task.

From the get-go, we gathered a team of people from different strata of our church to form the community building team. They strategised how to renovate the church building in ways that would both reflect our biblical principles and begin cultivating these values in the church community at the same time. To involve the rest of the church, we formed other interest groups from each different ministry. Each one was tasked to filter their ministry praxis through our five core values. Our congregation responded mostly positively. They were glad that we were not paying lip service to church values, but attempting to put into practice what we preached over the pulpit! To help the church understand the basis for these values, we ran short talks, discussions, and seminars in the initial years. Our "Dinner and Dialogues" sessions, where we facilitated conversations about our different core values over home-cooked meals, were the most helpful. These sessions were more than just fellowship; they were a collective space for us to use our five core values as a filter to ponder important issues. In the end, those who participated were not only able to understand the truth undergirding these values, but also internalise them.

Challenges on the Journey

During the construction process, we struggled the most with communicating effectively. As a result of mismatched expectations and misunderstandings, various groups ended up being frustrated with each other. Our leadership laboured through this to cultivate a culture of conversation, where we would work out our differences instead of burying conflict. We also modelled this culture by altering the way we received negative feedback ourselves. We recognised that "negative" feedback was at times simply "different" feedback and so did not waste energy being defensive. Instead, we intentionally created communication platforms to hear these other ideas. By listening first, and then deciding later whether to agree or respectfully disagree, we allowed everyone to feel heard and respected. These initial breakdowns in communication reminded us that everyone would embrace these core values at a different pace, and we needed to take the time to walk with those who were still on their way.

During the renovation, we also chose to continue using the church rather than move out. Our decision came in part from the advice of our Transition Interest Group, which had studied the biblical basis for "transition" inspired by the Festival of Booths. Despite having their own homes, the Israelites had stayed in booths to remember their journey through the wilderness with God. It was also their way of acknowledging that they were ultimately pilgrims utterly reliant on God while they lived on this earth. The temporal discomfort also reminded them of the importance of obedience as a people. These reflections on the significance of the Festival shaped our attitude towards our renovation process. We chose to stay in the building while it was being rebuilt as a form of meditation on the same pilgrim status and reliance on God that the Festival of Booths was intended to instil. Our architect ascertained that it was certainly possible, albeit inconvenient. At one point, we did not even have a functioning car park! Instead of enjoying the comforts of a rented facility, these inconveniences spurred us to appreciate all the other comforts in life even more. Space was a premium commodity and, during that season, we did our best to share, give up our rights to a room in order to honour another ministry, and be creative with our resources. We carpooled. We did our Bible studies at coffee-shops and had our fellowship gatherings in members' homes. We wanted to make use of this period to learn about being God's pilgrims as well as experience God's goodness. As we bore with the inconveniences and witnessed the gradual transformation of the building together, the entire church felt integrally involved in the renovation process. Staying back was the right decision.

We also had several practical decisions to consider. Several ideas—such as harvesting and reusing rainwater, as well as installing solar panels—had to be shelved because we could not afford it at the time. Also, in order to recycle our old equipment and materials responsibly, we had to plan ahead to incorporate these processes into our contractors' tight schedules. This required good organisation beforehand.

Getting the church to re-examine the way we lived was also initially trying. At times, we even bordered on being offensive to them. One Christmas lunch, we inadvertently pushed the BYO message too far and people thought we were saying, "If you don't bring your own cutlery, then don't eat!" That was a critical lesson for us. We realised that effecting change within the community cannot occur through an overbearing, judgmental, or holier-than-thou posture. Rather, we had to hold our idealism in tension with a realistic and gracious acceptance that people take time to change. Otherwise, our zeal to convince the church to participate in creation care could quickly slip into legalism.

As we remembered that creation care is meant to be enjoyed and embraced, we changed our approach. We gently welcomed the church to participate in this lifestyle through conversations and relationship building. For instance, we involved them in the creative repurposing of old furniture, particularly in upcycling some of our church pews. We partnered Ground-Up Initiative (GUI), a non-profit organisation that taught us how to refashion our pews into other kinds of furniture. Our old pews became benches, tables and partitions for office workstations while we used wood chips to fashion decorative pieces for our new building! As they immersed in the hands-on experience of repurposing our pews, and in sharing KPC's biblically-shaped motivation for doing this work with the team from GUI, our church community's belief in creation care began to grow naturally. Eight years later, it is so much a part of our DNA that church members now voluntarily opt for reusables despite the "inconvenience" of having to wash them after use. It has been even more gratifying to witness how the dishwashing points, which are integral to our church design, have become a space for conversations to occur and friendships to be built.

A Church for All His People

Our community building project has been a heuristic journey to disciple making; it shaped us to become a more generous and hospitable community. Given that renovation projects are highly energy consumptive, the leadership wanted to make full use of the resources that were poured into the project. One of the key ways to do this was to conceive of our church premises as an inclusive space that was welcoming and open to others—regardless of whether they were Christian or not.

Just a year before our building project was completed, a church approached our leadership to ask whether we would be open to sharing the church space with another congregation. We mooted the proposal to KPC during an EOGM, and were so encouraged when 94% of our congregation voted in favour of sharing! Right now, our premises are also being shared with another church community, a kindergarten, an exercise group, a taxi-driver fellowship, as well as some senior citizen and home-school groups.

We rejoice that the leadership's desire to share our building was embraced by our church community as well. Through our community building project journey, we have seen both the building and the people transformed.

This nine-year journey was a tremendous lesson for us. And yet, although the building has been completed, we want to keep learning or asking questions about how to be better stewards of our resources. God has given the gift of creation and we want to enjoy it gratefully and responsibly. We hope that our community can learn to hold on to the material things lightly, and to use whatever resources we have to bless those around us. We want to live out our five values more fully and creatively, and be a transforming missional community.

Paying Attention in the Anthropocene

Mary-Ruth Low

Mary-Ruth is a Malaysian who read Life Sciences at NUS before working in research and conservation, first radio-tracking reticulated pythons and later with urban wildlife while at the Singapore Zoo. In mid-2018 she chose to return to Malaysia, joining an NGO called Rimba. She works on fruit bat conservation and their role as pollinators. She finds deep meaning in work that helps people see the connectedness of this wonderful created world.

"This is what is wrong with the conservationist movement. It has a clear conscience. The guilty are always other people, and the wrong is always somewhere else."[1] ~Wendell Berry

When people ask me what I do, I usually say I work in "conservation". But as with so many labels, the term comes with its own set of baggage. Admittedly, it is an attractive word: it conjures up an image of someone donned in khaki-coloured gear in the forest, at one with nature, saving the animals, plants and fungi from human-caused destruction. The whole concept is often couched in fighting terms: "defending the rainforest in the war against land grabbers", "the armed struggle against ivory-poaching mafia", etc. The notion also comes with a sense of urgency: big international NGOs blast warnings of how few tigers, rhinos and elephants remain, how several football field-sized forests are cleared every hour, how our oceans are being fished to death, how the Great Pacific Garbage Patch is three times the size of France…and on and on it goes.

I did not exactly imagine I would end up stuck in this ginormous conservation impasse. I started out working life bright-eyed and bushy-tailed, in the bubble of academia. Then I joined the zoo as a conservation officer, where I was allowed a broader vantage point into the complexities and dynamics of the international conservation network. I had the privilege of meeting people who had dedicated their lives to this work, but it was also where I learned that

---

[1] Wendell Berry, "Why I am Not Going to Buy a Computer," in *What are People For? Essays by Wendell Berry* (San Francisco, CA: North Point Press, 1990),176.

conservation has a hundred different definitions and people are rarely on the same page as to how to go about it. I also learned (and struggled with the fact) that a lot of conservationists are angry at the rest of the human race, and yet have large egos and the occasional messiah complex.

It is no small irony that many of us, who rage against humanity, came from a starting point of wonder and amazement at the natural non-human world. I grew up in a family where the nightly entertainment meant watching a David Attenborough documentary. Despite his advanced age, Attenborough continues to inspire people through his measured and wonder-filled films. In his 2019 documentary series, *Our Planet*, he moves away from his usual "I stand in awe of unspoiled nature" message to a melancholic and heart-breaking showcase of a world affected by climate change. Despite all the awareness, many remain unreached, unmoved. How then do we deal with this precious, fragile state of our world, already broken and breaking so much more?

We attribute (a euphemism for "blame") most of the environmental issues today to "anthropogenic"—or human-caused—effects, so much so that this current geological age is referred to as the Anthropocene. It is not uncommon to hear a joke about how it would be good for the planet if humans died out. Attenborough once said in an interview that "we are a plague on earth".[2] How should we respond to these worldviews, as we attempt to be faithful image-bearers and care for non-human creation that is God's own?

---

2 Louise Gray, "David Attenborough—Humans Are Plague On Earth," *Telegraph*, Jan. 22, 2013, https://www.telegraph.co.uk/news/earth/earthnews/9815862/Humans-are-plague-on-Earth-Attenborough.html.

My current work involves the conservation of fruit bat pollinators, including flying foxes which are giant fruit bats with wingspans of up to two metres. Research has shown that bats pollinate durian, and without them to carry out this task of transferring pollen from one flower to another (on another tree), many durian lovers across Southeast Asia would have plenty to mourn about. The problem is this: the bats' roles as pollinators are unacknowledged and unrecognised, thus their conservation is not a priority. To make matters worse, these bats live in forests, which are being cut down to make way for durian plantations, the favoured monoculture crop of the day, fuelled by the burgeoning market in China. The work of conserving these bats then includes having to engage durian consumers, farmers, traders, and plantation managers. The way forward is not to obliterate humans from this planet. It is to get humans to see the connections, and how they can help.

This slow, relational work is sometimes sniffed at, even within conservation circles, simply because bats are not sexy like tigers or polar bears (no offense to them!). Yet, human engagement is how I believe bats will be saved. Instead of feeling helpless and hopeless in tackling the global extinction crisis, we can work out connections and help people (and ourselves along the way) join the dots.

What about us in urban centres such as Singapore and KL whose habitat is concrete? We may travel the world, be familiar with wildlife seen on BBC's *Blue Planet* and *Dynasties*, yet live estranged from our very own landscapes and natural heritage. How shall we address our ecological homelessness? The conventional conception of "creation care" as stewardship of the natural environment may be inadequate and incomplete for us to be faithful to *place*.

Let us come home to where God has called us and see our "emplaced-ness" as *gift*.

Miranda Harris, co-founder of A Rocha, often says that before we even get to choose the communities we want to identify with, first and foremost we *belong* to the Creator and the "created community". She encourages us, "We don't need to join a community or start a community. We need to look around us, identify, describe and embrace the one that God has already placed us in".[3] I believe that this "homecoming" and ontology of belonging for us who have no humus to tend to, no vast tracts of hinterland or living indigenous knowledge systems, can be expressed through thinking and acting *local*. Could we tend to our displacement? Can we identify the birds in our neighbourhood by their song? Can we learn the names of the trees we pass by everyday? Do we know where our food comes from or what happens when we throw our trash? In our Father's world, there is no "away". This world *is* our home, indeed, home to all of God's creatures, for he has made a covenant with every living thing (Genesis 8). How do we nurture affection and love for our home? Poet Mary Oliver says it simply, "To pay attention, this is our endless and proper work". Let us pay sacred attention.

---

3 Miranda Harris, "At Home in Creation", November 2013, BMS World Mission, MPEG-4, 21:31, https://vimeo.com/80892263.

The Biodiversity of Singapore

Note: Crustaceans include crabs, shrimp, copepods and amphipods; molluscs include snails, slugs, octopi and squid; chelicerates comprise of spiders and ticks; while mammals also include humans, domestic dogs and tapirs (which are known to occasionally swim over from Malaysia!)

Singapore consists of its mainland—Pulau Ujong—along with 54 smaller islands, comprising a total of 718 km², a quarter of which is reclaimed land. It is incredible that its biodiversity continues to persist, despite the intense urbanisation and landscape change. The nature reserves harbour endemic species—ones that can only be found in Singapore and nowhere else—including a tiny thumbnail-sized freshwater crab (*Johora singaporensis*) only known from three streams within Singapore!

Urban wildlife also abound, we have otters, common palm civets, long-tailed macaques, pythons, and even Sunda pangolins that share the same space as human residents! Many birders also come to Singapore specifically to see the Straw-headed Bulbul (*Pycnonotus zeylanicus*). Classified as Endangered under the IUCN Red List because of poaching pressures for the song bird trade, Singapore is recognised as one of the last remaining population strongholds for this species.

In 1863, Folliott S. Pierpoint was wandering through the peaceful English countryside where the beauty inspired him to reflect on God's gifts to his people, both in creation and in the Church. As he thought of Christ's salvific work for the redemption of creation, he penned the lyrics of perhaps one of the most well-loved English hymns, "For the Beauty of the Earth".

Today, even with only 4.7% of Singapore devoted to protected nature areas,[1] the beauty of creation is still all around us if we care to pay attention. We often fail to stop and smell the flowers of tembusu trees in bloom, pause to hear the song of the bulbuls or consider the starry sky. Our relationship with creation is often defined by

---

[1] "5th National Report to the Convention on Biological Diversity (2010-2014)", National Parks Board Singapore 2015, accessed Dec. 5, 2019, https://www.cbd.int/doc/world/sg/sg-nr-05-en.pdf.

utilitarian terms. Asians identify fish species at aquariums we visit in terms of food ("Best when steamed Hong Kong style!"). Perhaps the only chickens that children see are those at KFC. And has nature become a mere backdrop that will look cool in a selfie? Yet, "The world is *charged* with the grandeur of God"[2] (italics added) wrote Gerard Manley Hopkins. Let this extravagant beauty humble us. Let the scales fall from our eyes!

Begin a practice of recognising nature's beauty in our city. May it be our call to worship the Creator with the rest of creation. And may we mirror God in rejoicing in his handiwork (Psalm 104:31).

---

2 Gerard Manley Hopkins, "God's Grandeur," *Poetry Foundation*, accessed Dec. 5, 2019, https://www.poetryfoundation.org/poems/44395/gods-grandeur.

Amphibian Diversity in Urban Parks: Attending to Creation in the City

Melissa Ong & Prarthini M. Selveindran
(Friends of A Rocha in Singapore)

Friends of A Rocha in Singapore, which was formed in 2009, grew out of an informal community of volunteers and supporters of A Rocha. It continues to initiate a local expression of creation care that was inspired by A Rocha's mission and values: Christian, conservation, community, cross-cultural, and cooperation.

Urban Biodiversity

> "Our worship and work and witness will be incomplete until our responsibility to conserve the glorious, God-given diversity of earth's creatures becomes second nature."[1] ~Peter Harris

Three of us came together initially to share our love for biodiversity. Mary-Ruth and Prarthi were both former student researchers in the National University of Singapore (NUS) and had a keen interest in herpetology (the branch of biology concerning reptiles and amphibians); Melissa was serving with A Rocha International in communications. We lamented over the lack of integration between faith and ecology within the local Church, and our general disconnect with creation in our urban society.

We were eager to bridge this gap. We knew we wanted to begin a hands-on conservation initiative. It had to be simple enough for children to take part in, something accessible for families and church groups to do on their own. We surrendered our desires to God and trusted him to point us in the right direction. After assessing what was already taking place in Singapore's nature groups and citizen science projects, to our surprise, we found an unexplored niche that matched our passion and gifts!

Our Project Goals

Our project had a two-fold objective: first, get Christians

---

[1] Peter Harris, "Why Conservation is a Gospel Issue," *A Rocha Blog*, Sept. 15, 2016, https://blog.arocha.org/en/why-conservation-is-a-gospel-issue/.

outdoors to appreciate the biodiversity with which God has entrusted us; second, contribute to Singapore's biodiversity data, while not duplicating the significant citizen science work conducted by others.

We designed a two-year project to document frog diversity in selected urban parks across Singapore. Doing a survey to ascertain the diversity of frogs would give the National Parks Board (NParks) and local scientists a clearer picture of the species we have right at our doorstep. This diversity count would serve as a resource and record for NParks to better care for our urban wildlife and manage the park. Furthermore, frogs are a good indicator species of the health of their environment since they live on both land and in water. They are sensitive to pollutants and are often the first to be affected by environmental changes in the local ecosystem. In other words, the data collected would provide a snapshot of how well our urban parks are doing.

We submitted this proposal to NParks, who gave us some suggestions regarding our project method and chosen parks. They also sponsored the launch of our project in January 2015, where we held a training session at the Botany Centre for our volunteers. We shared the purpose of our project with them, and taught them how to identify urban frogs and our survey methodology.

As most frog species are nocturnal, we carried out our surveys between 7.30 p.m. and 9.30 p.m. We equipped our volunteers with head-lamps sponsored by NParks and tasked them to scan the vegetation along water bodies to detect the frogs. They used a combination of sight (via spotting the frogs) and sound (via hearing frog calls) to determine the frog species in that park. A volunteer was designated to record all our findings during the survey. An example of our data sheet can be found in the Appendix. We surveyed a total of 25 parks in one year and revisited those parks in the following year.

Two Saturdays a month, we gathered about six volunteers and set out to the designated park for our survey. In the span of those two years, we encountered more than 10 frog species, along with other interesting critters, such as the Malayan colugo, oriental whip snakes, Asian swamp eels, an Australian redclaw crayfish, common palm civet cats and a black spitting cobra! The most common frog species we saw were the banded bullfrog, field frog, dark-sided chorus frog, and the ubiquitous Asian toad.

The diversity across parks varied greatly. Some parks only had a few Asian toads, while others—such as Springleaf Nature park—yielded seven species! On 28 July 2017, at Clementi Woods, we came across a frog species that we failed to identify, and which we had not seen in the previous year. They were tiny—merely the size of a thumbnail—and there were a great number of them around. Further research following the survey revealed that this was a new record for this species in that park, and only the second sighting of this species in Singapore![2] This species—the

---

2 Kelvin K. P. Lim & Law Ing Sind., "Greenhouse Frogs at Clementi Woods," *Singapore Biodiversity Records 2017*, Aug. 31, 2017, https://lkcnhm.nus.edu.sg/app/uploads/2017/09/sbr2017-103-104.pdf.

Greenhouse frog (native to Cuba and several islands in the Caribbean)—is an invasive species in Singapore with no prior evidence of an established population. This was one of our small contributions to Singapore's biodiversity records.

Challenges on the Journey

Learning about creation care cannot happen solely within four walls or in front of a screen. It's got to be *experienced*. We wanted urban Christians to encounter God's handiwork for themselves and cultivate a deeper connection with it. Our big dream was for churches to recognise creation care as a normal part of Christian discipleship. We hoped that they would adopt a local park in their neighbourhood, and integrate environmental education into their programmes.

It was a hard sell. For many, frogs had an 'ick' factor. Next, our surveys were mostly on Saturday evenings, a time-slot taken up by many Christian programmes. Finally, we faced a challenge with long-term commitment: most volunteers came just once or twice. We often scrambled to find volunteers in the week leading up to the survey. Our most frequent and enthusiastic volunteers were not Christians, and we were encouraged by them.

Our newbies found it tricky to spot the frogs, since their eyes were not yet trained to do so. They were amazed at how we could spot them from afar! We showed them how to use their headlamps to look for eye-shine (when the light hits the eyes of critters). Sometimes we could not see the frogs, but only hear them all around us. With practice, our volunteers had fun discerning the different calls and identifying the species.

The fortnightly discipline of "going frogging" became a welcomed practice to go out exploring parts of Singapore after dusk. Going out at night in nature areas "shed new light" on creation in our city for many folks. Hunting for frogs in the quiet of the night, away from life's hustle and bustle, forced us to slow down and become more sensitive to creation. "*Wah! Never see before!*", "*I didn't know Singapore got so much nature!*", "*This frog is so cute!*"—these sentiments pretty much sum up how our volunteers felt during the walks. The wonder and delight we experienced was infectious and kindled the natural curiosity and affinity for nature in our volunteers, both young and old. Many of them told us that after joining these walks, noticing frogs and other creatures became second nature to them. These moments of connectedness are healing for our relationship with creation. They help to correct our utilitarian view of nature and re-awaken us to the intrinsic value of creation.

Small Hops Forward

Our walks created a space for people to connect faith and ecology. We were able to share life and motivate young Christians. As they saw other Christians pursuing conservation, they felt affirmed that it was indeed a worthy calling to pursue. It was also a means of speaking hope into the environmental crisis with both Christian and non-Christian volunteers alike.

If you want to get your church or friends started on creation care, a frog walk is something you can do! It is low-cost and does not require much equipment. Just go out, torch in hand, and begin your adventure in nature! Let us know if you need our help!

> *What a wildly wonderful world, GOD!*
> *You made it all, with Wisdom at your side,*
> *made earth overflow with your wonderful creations.*
> (Psalm 104:24 MSG)

Nurturing Wonder-filled Children

Shai Kroeker

Shai grew up in a kampung in Singapore, a daughter of towgay farmers. Formerly a secondary school Humanities teacher, she now calls British Columbia home where she is serving at the A Rocha Canada Brooksdale Environmental Centre with her husband, Steve. She is living out her passion for the integration of creation care when teaching children and youth, engaging refugee and low-income families as well as seniors, and providing hospitality through the ministry of A Rocha in Surrey, BC.

Let's start with an imaginative exercise:

- Close your eyes.
- Think of a moment you enjoyed in God's beautiful creation. What were you doing?
- How were you feeling?

Did you begin to feel relaxed as you savoured the memory?

Try this exercise with the children in your family or community; what did they say?

In his 2005 groundbreaking book, *Last Child in the Woods*, American author Richard Louv brought to our attention how our children today are suffering from what he calls "Nature-Deficit Disorder". "Nature-deficit disorder is not a formal diagnosis, but a way to describe the psychological, physical, and cognitive costs of human alienation from nature, particularly for children in their vulnerable developing years."[1] As children spend less time outdoors, they do not know their place well enough to form a meaningful and reciprocal relationship with it. Hence, it is very unlikely that they will even care about what is going on in the environment around them. As a result of this detached attitude that is formed during early and middle childhood, both children and nature suffer: children are unable to "reap the psychological and spiritual benefits they can glean from nature",[2] while nature loses a generation that feels a kinship with it. Instead it is treated as a functional resource that

---

1 Richard Louv, *Last Child in the Woods: Saving our Children from Nature-Deficit Disorder* (Chapel Hill, NC: Algonquin Books, 2008), 36.

2 Ibid., 159.

is to be exploited for our human benefit. This becomes a vicious cycle: since these children have not personally experienced the beauty of creation, when they become adults, they will also not expose their children to the awe and wonder of nature, and so on. For this reason, Louv calls a child in nature an "endangered indicator species";[3] the health of children and the health of the earth are inseparable.

What Louv has described is definitely an alarming trend that I am witnessing in Canada too. We need to get our children outside playing, and even better if we join them! There is an increasing number of research studies on the positive socio-emotional and psychological impacts of being in the natural world, especially on children. I would like to share some of the insights from these studies, as well as from my own experience as an environmental educator at the A Rocha Canada Brooksdale Environmental Centre.

1. Creation helps de-stress and calm us.

Creation has many therapeutic properties! Among other things, exposure to sunlight increases our brain's release of serotonin. It boosts our mood and helps us feel calm and focused.[4] This is true for the children who have been coming to our day camps. Each day, we would get them to sit silently in creation by themselves for 20 minutes. They would either draw or write down their observations. Often, the children would tell us that this quiet time in creation is the highlight of their experience! Also, as a first-time mother, I

---

3 Ibid.

4 Alexandra Sifferlin, "The Healing Power of Nature," *Time*, July 14, 2016, https://time.com/4405827/the-healing-power-of-nature/.

am so thankful that when my baby is fussing, I can always count on her calming down when I bring her outside and take a short walk in creation.

2. Creation develops and sharpens observation skills.

Children blossom when they have the chance to explore creation freely. Instead of telling them what to see and rattling off textbook facts, honour children by letting them exercise their innate observation skills in creation. It piques their curiosity, helps them make connections on their own, and cultivates self-directed learning.

3. Creation develops and sharpens creativity.

As children learn to recognise that no one thing in creation is exactly the same, they discover that God is a very creative Maker. When left to unstructured free play in creation, they instinctively express their creativity. Children often make something out of the natural elements they find during their play. Many modern inventions have taken inspiration from nature to solve problems through biomimicry or biomimetics, like velcro and colour displays for e-readers.

4. Exploring creation helps us to stay healthy physically and emotionally.

Many studies have shown that obesity is on the rise in children. As they become more addicted to their electronic devices or virtual reality, they prefer to stay indoors.[5] These

---

5 According to the World Health Organization (WHO), "Childhood obesity is one of the most serious public health challenges of the 21st century. The problem is global and is steadily affecting many low- and middle-income countries, particularly in urban settings. Moreover, its prevalence has increased at an alarming rate. Globally, in 2016 the number of overweight children under the age of 5 was estimated to be

sedentary habits that are set early in life tend to follow children through adolescence and adulthood, putting them on a path to obesity and a whole host of other chronic health problems.

Research indicates that exposure to nature can act as a protective factor for the mental health of young people.[6] A recent study of 29,784 Canadian adolescents found that engagement in outdoor play—even as little as a half hour per week—was associated with decreased prevalence of psychological symptoms in females, and decreased prevalence of psychosomatic symptoms in both males and females of mental health disorders.[7] When children are exploring creation, they engage in a therapeutic multi-sensory experience. They are more likely to remain active into adulthood, and report higher levels of physical, mental, and spiritual well-being.[8]

---

over 41 million. Almost half of all overweight children under 5 lived in Asia and one quarter lived in Africa." Taken from https://www.who.int/dietphysicalactivity/childhood/en/. Accessed on Nov. 14, 2019.

"Inactivity is a big part of the problem. According to a 2018 report from the WHO, more than 23 percent of adults and 81 percent of teens worldwide do not get enough physical activity." Taken from https://www.who.int/news-room/fact-sheets/detail/physical-activity. Accessed on Nov. 14, 2019.

6   Louv, *Last Child*, 323. Leyla E. McCurdy, Kate E. Winterbottom, Suril S. Mehta, James R. Roberts, "Using Nature and Outdoor Activity to Improve Children's Health," *Current Problems in Pediatric and Adolescent Health Care* 40, no. 5 (July 2010): 102–117.

7   Caroline Piccininni, Valerie Michaelson, Ian Janssen & William Pickett, "Outdoor Play and Nature Connectedness as Potential Correlates of Internalized Mental Health Symptoms among Canadian Adolescents," *Preventive Medicine* 112(2018): 168–175.

8   Madhuleena Roy Chowdhury, "The Positive Effects of Nature on

Explore creation together as a family, and encourage your children to do so with their friends. Singapore's hot and humid weather is often cited as a reason for not being active outdoors, but there are means to mitigate this! Try going out in the early mornings or after dusk, or dressing in UV protective clothing to make outdoor adventures more enjoyable. Learning exciting facts about Singapore's unique biodiversity can also pique your child's interest in exploring creation. (Did you know that tiny Singapore has more tree species than the whole of the North American continent?)

5. Creation boosts learning in children by providing a more supportive context for learning.

Children who have attention difficulties in the classroom or learning challenges, such as attention deficit hyperactivity disorder (ADHD), may thrive by learning in creation. In my work, I have seen many children with learning disabilities truly blossom when they learn in the forest, by the river or in our organic garden. Unlike a traditional classroom setting, they are able to observe things and make connections between what they see. This helps them focus better and become more confident.

I fondly remember my experience with a fifth grader whom I led on a forest walk. He had gotten off the bus looking disinterested and disgruntled, and I was sure I was going to have a hard time with him. To my surprise, he was so engaged and started pointing out things in the forest that even I did not notice! He became the natural leader of the group,

---

Your Mental Well-Being," *Positive Psychology*, accessed Oct. 24, 2019, https://positivepsychology.com/positive-effects-of-nature/.

peer-teaching his friends and sharing information that I had just taught them. At the end of the activity, his face shone and his eyes lit up when I affirmed his learning and leadership abilities. As I walked with the class to the bus, I made sure I gave the teacher feedback about him. She looked at me incredulously and exclaimed, "Thank you so much for telling me! He is usually the worst student in my class."

6. Creation connects us to the Creator.

It has always been God's desire for us to know him. Romans 1:20 tells us, "For since the creation of the world God's invisible qualities—his eternal power and divine nature—have been clearly seen, being understood from what has been made, so that people are without excuse." In other words, God deliberately made his "invisible qualities" tangible through "what has been made"—i.e. his natural world—so that his people would have a way to know and understand him. Our urban society's tendency to be disconnected from creation is thus even more troubling. As my pastor once said, "When we lose touch with creation, we lose touch with the Creator."

In the 2014 Living Planet Report by the World Wildlife Fund for Nature (WWF), out of more than 150 analysed, Singapore had the seventh-largest ecological footprint (a measurement of a population's demands on natural resources) in the world. In the 2012 report, we ranked 12th. While much more must be done to reduce our ecological footprint, there is still hope. As the Church and the body of Christ, we can make a difference if we faithfully practice wise stewardship of the environment. We can begin to reduce our ecological footprint by educating our church family about creation care. We can highlight pertinent issues, such as the carbon emissions of our flights,[9] food waste, and the use of disposables. We can also explore how to make more sustainable choices, like using less plastic, or opting for more eco-friendly and sustainably-sourced products. As children of God, made lovingly in his image (Genesis 9:6), God has given us the mandate to be his image-bearers here on this earth and to look after the world as he himself would do. We show the world that we love God by loving his creation and this allows us to engage people in hearing the gospel creatively.

It is crucial for the Church to introduce the natural world to its younger generation, both for their physical *and* spiritual benefits. As theologian and creation care advocate Steven Bouma-Prediger said, "We care for only what we love. We love only what we know. We truly know only what we experience."[10] Therefore, one of the best ways to help our children cultivate a love for creation is through experiential outdoor learning, which we can do even during Sunday school! Depending on the surroundings of the church, one can bring children out to observe the flora and fauna in the neighbourhood. Different experiential learning activities can be tailored for different age groups. If the church

---

9 Consider carbon offsetting holiday travels and mission trips with Climate Stewards (climatestewards.org), part of the A Rocha network, which supports community forestry, water filter and cookstove projects in the developing world.

10 Steven Bouma-Prediger, *For the Beauty of the Earth: A Christian Vision for Creation Care*, 2nd ed. (Grand Rapids, MI: Baker Academic, 2010), 21.

compound is devoid of vegetation, a community garden with raised beds is another way of exposing children to creation. It will become an engaging space for the children to learn about the amazing way that God creates life from seed to fruit, the valuable ethics of tending a garden, and to appreciate how food is grown. It never fails to bring me joy to witness countless children visiting A Rocha exclaim at the sweetness of our organically-grown fresh vegetables, like kale or broccoli flowers! Many parents are so surprised by the kids' sudden love for greens. They say, "You never eat this at home!" As adults, tilling the soil and tending to the garden bring the parables of Jesus to life and enrich them with new meaning. The benefits of having a community garden in a church are quite far ranging!

Through outdoor experiential learning, the Church can help both children and adults develop a deep relationship with God. This creates a life-giving cycle that reverses the nature-deficit disorder spiral that I highlighted at the start of my article. The more we learn to love creation, the more we will love God, which will, in turn, lead us to love creation even more, and so on. As Martin Luther wisely said, "Now if I believe in God's Son and remember that he became man, all creatures will appear a hundred times more beautiful to me than before. Then I will properly appreciate the sun, the moon, the stars, trees, apples, as I reflect that he is Lord over all things."

***

Psalm 24:1 proclaims that "The earth is the Lord's and everything in it". If we love God, then we should love all that belongs to Him, for He loves all His creation. Venture outside to rediscover the awe and wonder of His creation! Have fun exploring and may you grow in your relationship with God and creation!

FURTHER READING

1. Christopher Bergland, "8 Eye-Opening Ways Kids Benefit from Experiences with Nature," *Psychology Today*, Mar.18, 2019, https://www.psychologytoday.com/intl/blog/the-athletes-way/201903/8-eye-opening-ways-kids-benefit-experiences-nature.

2. Richard Louv, *Children and Nature Network*, https://www.childrenandnature.org, accessed Oct. 24, 2019. This is an American based network that features various nature projects from around the world. Our NParks' initiative of a new biophilic playground at HortPark was even given a noteworthy mention!

3. "Green Living Resources," *A Rocha Environmental Stewardship*, accessed Nov. 15, 2019, https://arocha.ca/get-involved/green-living-resources/.

4. *The Sayang List: Conserving 10 Threatened Species in Singapore* (Singapore: WWF-Singapore), accessed Nov. 15, 2019, https://www.wwf.sg/our_work/living_planet_report_2018_/.

5. *The Living Planet Report 2018*, accessed Nov. 15, 2019, http://wwf.panda.org/knowledge_hub/all_publications/living_planet_report_2018/#.

For more resources on Green Living, check out: https://arocha.ca/get-involved/green-living-resources/.

COMMUNITY IS A LOT LIKE A GARDEN

Priscilla Teh

Priscilla is a final-year Geography student in NUS and has been a volunteer with Friends of A Rocha in Singapore since 2016. Drawn towards nature and animals from a young age, she cherishes her morning runs and walking her dog, Nala. She calls Bethesda Pasir Ris Mission Church her faith community, where she is currently mentoring a group of girls (now ages 15–16) whom she has had the privilege of journeying through life with since they were 12–13 years old.

An Intern at A Rocha Canada

It all started with a prayer, "God, what is your big plan for the earth? How may I bring together my love for animals, teaching, and my faith?" That was when God showed me a part of his kingdom work called creation care and led me to A Rocha,[1] an international Christian organisation engaging communities in nature conservation. I wanted so much to immerse myself in the theology and practice of earth-keeping, that I joined the team at the A Rocha Canada Brooksdale Environmental Centre in British Columbia as an environmental education (EE) intern in the summer of 2018.

Together with interns from the Sustainable Agriculture and Conservation Science programmes, we lived, worked and ate in community on a beautiful 18-acre property with forests, a threatened river system, organic gardens, and heritage houses. My role was to assist veteran educator Ruth Des Cotes in the planning and running of experiential EE programmes for the local community, which included school groups, refugees, and senior citizens.

---

[1] A Rocha responds to the global crisis of biodiversity loss by carrying out community-based conservation projects. Through residential field study centres, site-based projects and wider advocacy, A Rocha carries out ecological monitoring and research in areas of high value for wildlife; spearheads practical measures for conserving and restoring habitats and their fauna and flora; encourages appreciation of nature and participation in its conservation, through environmental education and community outreach; and provides a forum for understanding the relevance of the Christian faith to environmental issues. The story of A Rocha is told in Peter Harris' *Under the Bright Wings* (Bellingham, WA: Regent College Publishing, 2000) and *Kingfisher's Fire: A Story of Hope for God's Earth* (Oxford, UK: Monarch Books, 2008).

One of things I really enjoyed was taking the children (between the ages of 7 to 9) pond dipping at our thriving wetland. Using nets, they would gather creatures and observe them in trays. These city children were always so fascinated by the critters they found—bullfrog tadpoles, dragonfly nymphs, pumpkinseed fish, among others. I would also bring the children out on our forest trail to learn about nature through playing games. They truly came alive when they explored creation and met our farm animals, especially when they petted the chickens!

Living as God's Created Community

We belong to God's created community of love, which includes human and non-human creation. As such, community is one of A Rocha's core values. Living and working in community at A Rocha centres is a powerful experience for many interns and long-term volunteers. Community is also a mirror. In sharing life together with 14 interns of diverse backgrounds, and being far from the familiar contexts where I am known, I had to lay down my identity and surrender the things I had placed my self-worth in. That vulnerability that I felt led me to a greater acceptance of myself and my fellow interns, and appreciation for the beauty in each person I encountered at A Rocha.

We cooked, learned to bake sourdough bread, and brewed kombucha together. The sustainable agriculture interns harvested diverse produce fresh from our farm that we cooked up—funky-shaped carrots, organic flavourful tomatoes, zucchini, kale—as we broke bread together. It was my first time eating food from our land. I had never seen how broccoli, zucchini or tomatoes grew; they were so healthy and huge! This holistic farm-to-table experience was so very different from eating vegetables from NTUC: veggies wrapped in plastic that have travelled many miles. Through this, I became more conscious of Singapore's consumerist culture—how quick we are to buy and throw away, or to purchase something out of convenience rather than make it from scratch. I began to recognise the value of things and appreciate the people who made them even more. It felt good to know who grew the food I ate, and know and love the place it had come from. I gained a deeper understanding of what I was putting in my body and a deeper gratitude for food.

What Does Creation Care Mean to Me?

In my desire to share this way of living out creation care, I was inspired to start a community garden in my church. I asked an elder if I could have the unused sand pit near our kindergarten to grow vegetables and flowers. I wanted it to embody the spirit of Brooksdale Environmental Centre, a gentle way of inviting people, especially children, to participate in creation care as a way of life and an important part of our faith. The leaders were excited about it and, with the help of many in the church, this garden became a reality in 2019!

Creation care is an expression of my love for our God and for our neighbour, as well as a way I put into action my longing for ecological justice in the world. While I am confronted daily by what seems to be the insurmountable systemic exploitation of the earth and of the world's poorest people, my caring for creation comes not from a position of anxiety, futility or resignation. Rather, it stands firmly on the hope that is in Christ, and on the joy of being part of God's restoration and renewal of the whole cosmos. On a personal level, I cherish creation for the way it ministers to me. It has been a teacher and a big part of my spiritual formation. It is my desire to help people experience the wonder of creation and its Creator, and to spur them to join this ministry of reconciliation.

"Community is a lot like a garden," says Jonathan Wilson-Hartgrove in *New Monasticism*.[2] We make the mistake of seeing church as a repair shop, and people as broken and in need of fixing. But we are not problems to be fixed. What we need is to "tend" to a culture of grace and truth. Tending a garden is a long and messy process. In the same way, we are called to tend "the soil" of our communities (and our world) and trust the Spirit to bring life within it. It is my hope that as we tend to our little church garden, and to each other, that we can witness and delight in the interconnectedness of God's creation. May his will be done on earth, as it is in heaven.

---

[2] Jonathan Wilson-Hartgrove, *New Monasticism: What It Has to Say to Today's Church* (Grand Rapids, MI: Brazos Press, 2008).

Various translations of Genesis 1:26 render *dominion* as "rule over" (NASB, NIV), "have dominion over" (KJV, NRSV), "reign over" (NLT). These hermeneutical developments together with the paucity of Christian theological reflection on the role and value of the non-human creation have influenced the manner with which we exercise our stewardship over the rest of God's creation.

God's purpose for humanity in Genesis 1 and 2 was (and is) to "have dominion", "to rule over," but this picture is incomplete without Genesis 2:15, where God puts humanity in the Garden of Eden "to work it and take care of it" (NIV), "tend" (NLT), "cultivate and keep it" (NASB). To rule and to have dominion is only appropriate when humanity reflects the kind of rule and dominion that God himself extends to us. It has a direct correlation with the premise that humanity is made in the very likeness of God and we are to reflect the kind of King that God is, one who takes the form of a servant and lays his life down for his creation (Philippians 2: 7-8). Humanity is likewise mandated to mirror that rule over creation and surrender our dominion to God's dominion. Just as God is the self-giving Creator, mankind is to reflect that caretaker role in serving and keeping God's Garden.

Finances, Social Justice & Climate Action: A Paradoxical Approach

Eunice Ng

Eunice's research focus is in the interface between corporate strategy and sustainability. Her research studies examine managerial decision-making in response to paradoxes in corporate sustainability. Prior to pursuing her PhD in strategic management, Eunice was an audit senior at a Big Four accounting firm, working on audit engagements in the luxury retail, manufacturing, and medical industries. As a mama to a little girl, Eunice grapples with the paradoxical demands of work, life, and living out creation care every day.

> *He has told you, O man, what is good;*
> *and what does the Lord require of you*
> *but to do justice, and to love kindness,*
> *and to walk humbly with your God?*
>
> Micah 6:8 (ESV)

Our financial assets give us the power to mitigate climate change as well as enact social justice and equity. However, the ethos of maximizing profits and self-interests tends to dominate the way both leaders of business corporations and individuals make financial decisions. In order to create sustainable development that is inclusive and equitable, we need to transform how we use and generate wealth. It is critical that we consider the principles of financial stewardship that God requires of us as His disciples in such a time as this.

Descriptive: Developments on Corporate Sustainability in Singapore

Singapore's stock exchange—Singapore Exchange—joined the global trend of stock exchanges in mandating all publicly listed companies to issue a sustainability report on a "comply or explain" basis for financial years on and after 31 December 2017.[1] In addition, Singapore's government implemented the Carbon Pricing Act on 1 January 2019, with plans to increase the carbon tax rate in the near

---

1 "Corporate Social Responsibility Disclosure Efforts by National Governments and Stock Exchanges," *Initiative for Responsible Investment*, Cambridge, MA: Harvard Kennedy School, accessed Nov. 5, 2018, http://iri.hks.harvard.edu/files/iri/files/corporate_social_responsibility_disclosure_3-27-15.pdf.

future.[2] These regulations have sent a signal to both public and private companies that there needs to be greater transparency and accountability in environmental, social, and governance issues. Within the business sector in Singapore, managerial attitudes towards corporate sustainability vary. While some business managers merely perceive this as a compliance exercise, others recognise the urgency to improve their firms' sustainability performance. Yet, whether or not they do so because they genuinely believe in the cause or because they believe that these initiatives ultimately lead to superior financial success for their firm is another story. For some, underlying this "business case for sustainability" logic is a belief that environmental preservation and human welfare are still secondary to wealth generation. Such an approach perceives environmental and social pursuits as merely means to an economic prosperity end.

As individuals, how we spend our money can also inherently reflect that we value our self-interests over the welfare of others or the earth. We may default to single-use items for the sake of convenience despite the significant environmental cost, or consume fast fashion without considering the labour conditions to which workers along the manufacturing supply chains are subjected.

Normative: What can be with business and finance

While these notions have been the dominant paradigm among business leaders and academic scholars, Christians

---

[2] "Carbon Tax," *National Environmental Agency*, accessed Nov. 16, 2019, https://www.nea.gov.sg/our-services/climate-change-energy-efficiency/climate-change/carbon-tax.

need to consider if this is aligned with biblical values.

In conversations with Christians, I hear people say that God gave humankind dominion over creation (in reference to Genesis 1:26), and therefore creation should serve the needs of man. Underlying this reasoning is an authoritarian perspective that justifies the exploitation of natural resources for the benefit of self. They also often reason that the focus should be on generating wealth before one can accumulate sufficient resources to do charitable works. Yet, the means by which we generate that wealth may ironically be to the detriment of others or the earth. Their justification for this is that this earth will pass away and we will have a new earth anyway (in reference to Revelation 21:1 and Isaiah 65:17). Climate action is rarely discussed or done.

What if we realise that the environmental impacts arising from how we use and generate wealth is inextricably linked with the health of our planet and the well-being of others, especially the poor and the disadvantaged?[3] With this in mind, how can Christians change the way we and the organisations that we lead or work for use and generate wealth? How do we reconcile this with loving others as Christ has loved us (John 13:34), or with doing justice, loving mercy, and walking humbly with our God (Micah 6:8)?

There is an emerging view within management scholars that pursuing economic, environmental, and social

---

3 "The Rich, the Poor and the Future of the Earth: Equity in a Constrained World, 2012," *Christian Aid*, accessed Oct. 24, 2019, https://reliefweb.int/sites/reliefweb.int/files/resources/constrained-world.pdf.

objectives with equal importance is possible when business leaders adopt a paradoxical mindset.[4] Individuals with this mindset are energised by pursuing contradictory goals, as they recognise that accepting contradictions is essential for their success. This requires us to approach financial profitability and other sustainability issues (e.g. preserving our natural environment, protecting the well-being of others, future generations) as intrinsically valuable.[5] When we accept, even value, the tensions that arise from conflicting financial and environmental/social concerns, we are then able to search for "both/and" strategies that can effectively address competing demands. With that, the corporation becomes multi-objective, engaging the diverse goals of various stakeholders and being more than merely a wealth generator.

Our relationship with God guides this thought process. Following His heart demands that we run counter to dominant beliefs and values that do not align with His Word (James 1:27). It requires us to turn from the sole pragmatism of "what's in it for me or my business?" (Philippians 2:4) and explore the corporate and individual contributions we can make toward sustainable and equitable development beyond economic profit.

---

[4] Ella Miron-Spektor, Amy Ingram, Josh Keller, Wendy K. Smith & Marianne W. Lewis, "Microfoundations of Organizational Paradox: The Problem is How We Think about the Problem," *Academy of Management Journal* 61 no. 1, (2018): 26–45.

[5] Tobias Hahn, Frank Figge, Jonatan Pinkse & Lutz Preuss, "A Paradox Perspective on Corporate Sustainability: Descriptive, Instrumental, and Normative Aspects," *Journal of Business Ethics* 148, no. 2, (2018): 235–248.

Prescriptive: What can we possibly do?

This section aims to inspire our first steps forward in reconsidering how we use our financial assets.

Board of directors and investors: Your response as a board director or an investor can change the organisational cultures and governance structures that regulate managerial decision-making over corporate sustainability. Here are some ways in which you can make those changes:

- Engage company management and board directors on firms' environmental and social performances and related issues.
- Equip yourself with knowledge on various environmental and social issues of the firms you govern, and also sustainability developments within the broader system.
- Recognise that you can make significant impact with your wealth:
  - Review carefully the companies you invest in. (Are you directly/indirectly funding companies with business models/activities that carry high environmental/social costs?)
  - Consider shifting your investments into companies that contribute to more sustainable and equitable development.
  - Consider new financial instruments such as green bonds (that are used to fund projects with positive environmental benefits).

Business leaders: Instead of viewing environmental and

social performances as sub-categories under financial performance (or even non-existent dimensions), consider them as independent and equally important firm performance dimensions. You should work to:

- Identify sustainability goals, targets, and develop measurement indicators relevant to your firm's context.
- Include environmental and social impact assessments as key criteria into your strategic decision-making matrix.
  - Identify relevant United Nations Sustainable Development Goals for your firm's context so as to develop proper frameworks to respond to sustainability issues.
- Communicate the imperative and urgency for substantive action on corporate sustainability with your stakeholders.
  - Communication should go beyond board directors and shareholders to include your firms' value networks, such as your employees and supply chain partners.
- Identify opportunities to collaborate and co-create strategies with your stakeholders on corporate sustainability issues.
  - Be willing to invest resources (e.g. financial, human, knowledge) in educating suppliers to change their sustainability practices substantially.
  - Participate in cross-sector partnerships with other stakeholders to facilitate the spread of knowledge and practices.

Individuals: The most important and first step forward we can take is to reduce our personal consumption. In addition, we ought to:

- Collectively change our consumption habits and preferences to integrate environmental/social concerns, such that companies will naturally respond by changing their products accordingly.
- Explore ways to reduce collective environmental impacts in the organisations that we interact with.
- Advocate and make environmental/social concerns salient within our organisations.

A Brief Note to the Church

Environmental sustainability is perhaps the least considered dimension within the Church in Singapore. Collectively, we have been more proactive in social and justice issues; we ensure finances are budgeted for evangelism efforts and caring for the poor, disadvantaged, and marginalised in society. Yet, there is a lack of recognition that the degradation of our natural environment has tangible impacts on the welfare of others, especially the poor or disadvantaged whom we desire to look out for. The cumulative waste that we generate from church events, gatherings, and camps can be astounding, which, ironically, is funded by the tithes and offerings that we collect. I hope that we, and especially the leadership of various congregations, can begin examining our environmental impact. We can seek to:[6]

---

[6] A Rocha UK's "Eco Church" programme can be a useful reference for us in our journey to integrate creation care into church life. Their free resources are available at https://ecochurch.arocha.org.uk/resources/.

- Intentionally encourage a culture of creation care across our members.
- Develop environmental policies and practices for our own congregations.
  - This could include radically eliminating single-use items within our church compounds and events.
- Integrate environmental impact assessment into our decision-making and operations.

Concluding Remarks

Our finances are a major channel through which we can do justice, love kindness, and walk humbly with our God. Let us align the way we use and generate wealth with the biblical values that we espouse to hold. May we be good stewards of what has been entrusted to us on this Earth, and reflect the life and light of Christ in this world through our financial wealth.

ACTION POINTS

Board directors and investors

1. Engage company management and board directors on firms' environmental and social performances and related issues.
2. Equip yourself with knowledge on various environmental and social issues of the firms you govern, and also sustainability developments within the broader system.
3. Review the companies within your investment portfolio and consider investing responsibly.

Business leaders

1. Identify sustainability goals, targets, and develop measurement indicators relevant to your firm's context.
2. Include environmental and social impact assessments as key criteria into your strategic decision-making matrix.
3. Communicate with your stakeholders on the imperative and urgency for substantive action on corporate sustainability.
4. Identify opportunities to collaborate and co-create strategies with your stakeholders on corporate sustainability issues.

Individual

1. Reduce your personal consumption and consume thoughtfully, starting from your home.
2. Explore ways to reduce collective environmental impacts in the organisations that we interact with.

3. Advocate and make environmental/social concerns salient within our organisations.

Church congregations
1. Intentionally encourage a culture of creation care across our members.
2. Develop environmental policies and practices for our own congregations.
3. Integrate environmental impact assessment into our decision-making and operations.

THINKING CHRISTIANLY ABOUT FOOD

Reuben Ang

Reuben grew up to love the local foodscape through experiences shared with his extended family of cooks and bakers. Formerly a campus staff-worker with the Fellowship of Evangelical Students (FES), he now manages his family's food service business, under the business group Hesed & Emet Holdings, which operates food courts and events catering businesses through heritage brands such as Elsie's Kitchen Catering. He is excited about serving God through kingdom businesses with missional impact in areas of addressing nutritional deficit among vulnerable communities, food waste management, and environmentally sustainable business operations.

Food, to me, stirs up a myriad of emotional experiences. A good meal can make my day as quickly as a poorly executed one can leave me grumpy. It also evokes fond childhood memories. I grew up in a family that was deeply immersed in the food business and spent my formative years around an abundance of good food. The sights and sounds in the kitchens of the family business, as well as countless family meals, formed memories that snowballed into something surprisingly educational.

My clan of old-school foodies had plenty to say about food. Every comment about what was going on in the kitchen that day or the passionate critiques of the dishes on the table became glimpses of the food ecosystem in which I was embedded. There were also opportunities to explore the entire food value-chain from farm to fork: my father exposed us to the inner workings of the food business from a young age by involving us in his daily procurement trips to the vegetable wholesale centre at midnight. It was inevitable that I, too, would eventually cultivate a passion for food!

During my time in university, and through the Varsity Christian Fellowship, I was pushed to explore a more holistic and integrated understanding of life and faith. I began seeing myself as a Christian who was participating in the momentum of God's ongoing redemptive and reconciling work. This meant that I could no longer solely focus on a transcendent reality in the distant future, but also in a redeemed here-and-now. As a business student, I asked myself: how could we operate a business shaped by a hopeful imagination of God's kingdom that was both already here and not yet?

Prior to joining the family's F&B business, I remember sitting in the University canteen baulking at how the F&B establishments served dine-in customers with disposable cutlery, just to save on dish washing. In my idealism, I recall promising myself that I would never participate in such wasteful behaviour. Yet, merely a month into the family business, I was shocked at how easily I assimilated the norms and "best practices" of the industry. The F&B sector's tight labour situation meant that even our in-house staff meals were supplied with disposable cutlery for convenience. We eventually changed that by introducing proper dining ware and employing stewarding staff in our canteen. This was the first of many "inconvenient" initiatives, done in the hope that the costs would balance themselves out. The road ahead would not promise easy answers; we just had to ask more questions.

With the bounty and variety of food we enjoy in Singapore, we scarcely give deeper thought to our food beyond when to grab our next meal or where best to satisfy our cravings. Our relative affluence gives (most of) us the choice of eating almost any type of produce from wherever, whenever, regardless of origin or seasonality. We could have Australian pork, American beef or Korean strawberries. But what about the ecological cost of this luxury? Shipping and freight transport have severe environmental impact on God's creation—including significant carbon emissions and pollution.

I was challenged to explore using local produce by a couple whose wedding menu I was planning. As a mass-market food service provider, our customers expect competitive pricing and a large variety in our menus. "Going local" would seriously restrict the ingredients available to us (Singapore currently grows only 10% of its food)[1] and increase costs by 4 to 10 times more than using the usual global channels. It would take considerable effort to educate consumers that this is a desirable alternative. Embarking on this journey to "go local" for a more sustainable alternative can be a costly exercise in discipleship that demands a complete re-look at our supply-chain and processes. Yet, our care for creation stems from a heart of obedience to the call to steward what God has created.

This also means that we are working to ensure that our international supplies are from sustainable sources. We often forget that there is a high cost in paying low prices, either to the environment (e.g., pollution from unsustainable practices) or to people further up the value-chain (e.g., suppressed wages or unjust working conditions). As part of our efforts, one recent change made was to switch our Vietnamese Sutchi Catfish ("Dory Fish") orders to an Aquaculture Stewardship Council (ASC) certified farm. While that would usually result in doubling costs compared to remaining with our existing local distributor, we managed to negotiate the prices down by going directly to the source and ordering in bulk. As the Singapore government aims to produce 30% of Singapore's nutritional needs locally by

---

[1] Aqil Haziq Mahmud, "Singapore aims to produce 30% of its nutritional needs by 2030, up from less than 10%," *CNA*, Mar. 7, 2019, https://www.channelnewsasia.com/news/singapore/singapore-produce-30-own-food-up-from-10-nutritional-needs-11320426.

2030 for food security reasons,[2] we eagerly anticipate an increase in sustainable sourcing options.

Looking ahead, my family business, Elsie's Kitchen, also intends to address the issue of food waste—both in terms of operationally reducing it, as well as proper disposal management. Food that is produced or purchased is sometimes wasted due to poor storage or excess procurement. Currently, NEA estimates 2.5kg of food a week is wasted by each household, equal to half of all household waste.[3] A quick look at unfinished meals at hawker centres tell only half the story. Once food goes into Singapore's waste management system, it ends up at incineration plants meant to reclaim energy back to the power grid. However, food waste (wet waste) is unrecyclable and only decreases the efficiency of incineration and energy reclamation. While minimal food waste is most ideal, the next best step is to properly sort waste prior to disposal. This enables food waste to be fed into composting digesters to be either reclaimed as compost or discharged into the sewage network. To do our part, we intend to perform food waste audits in our business operations. They will identify the by-products that can be incorporated back into the menu through creative menu planning, such as using watermelon rind to make delicious pickles.

---

2 Ibid.

3 Lim Min Zhang, "2.5kg of food a week wasted by each household, equal to half of all household waste: NEA study," *Straits Times*, Dec. 3, 2017, https://www.straitstimes.com/singapore/25kg-of-food-a-week-wasted-by-each-household-equal-to-half-of-all-household-waste-nea.

As a *missional* business, we endeavour to participate in the same momentum of what God is already doing in his creation—that is, God's mission of ushering in his kingly redemptive reign to save, heal, reconcile, restore, and make *all things* new (Revelation 21:5). Our journey to more sustainable business operations and creation care practices are adopted in the light of this kingdom. It is a kingdom reality that is filled with life and "very good" things (Genesis 1:31) that brings him Eden (lit. delight in Hebrew). This participation is also not a private affair, thus necessitating the invitation to our internal and external stakeholders to join us, facilitated through customer engagement and educational sessions. We continue to engage schools and customers through our factory tours and visits to share this vision that we may (hopefully) change lives and worldviews. Through all this, we testify to the reality of the whole gospel lived out. Practices adopted in our business, God-willing, offer glimpses of a reconciled world order because the King who died for all reigns over this business and over all that we do.

So, what can we do to think more Christianly about food? Here's a toolkit that will help you make small changes that can make a big impact.

Toolkit

10 things you could change about your relationship with food:

1. Know where your food comes from and how it was produced. Ask questions and research. Look for sustainability accreditation.

2. Explore what produce is grown locally and incorporate more of that into your diet; it is usually fresher but costs slightly more. Start befriending your local wet market stall holders. (Hint: mostly seafood and vegetables)

3. Be prepared to pay more. Remember there's sometimes a high cost to low prices.

4. Make a market list before buying food or produce at the supermarket so that you do not buy on impulse or over order.

5. Ask for reduced portions at food establishments and order only what you can consume. All-you-can-eat buffets hurt your waistline and encourage you to consume excessively.

6. Maintain your home chillers and freezers and keep a record of the internal temperature to ensure no food is wasted due to spoilage or clutter. (Chiller 0-4°C, Freezer < -12°C)

7. Dine-in more often or bring your own cutlery and take-away containers to reduce the usage of single-use plastics.

8. Sort your waste and dispose of them appropriately for recycling or incineration.
9. Set-up a small-scale vermicomposting system in your home to dispose of food waste.
10. Join a community of creative and like-minded individuals who can share creative recipes and food waste-saving ideas or form a food rescue group to share rescued produce with the community.

GOD UNCHANGING IN A CHANGING CLIMATE

Hoi Wen Au Yong

Hoi Wen is passionate about connecting nature, people, and faith. She works in the air transport sector to shape sustainability strategy and transform the business through environmental innovation and value creation. Previously, she was an environmental trainer, connecting children and adults to the beauty of God's creation through nature walks, farming and washing dishes! She's always up for a good cup of coffee, especially if it's organic and fairtrade.

Called to Environmental Action

Borneo, 1994. It was a bumpy ride as my family and I travelled on dirt tracks deep into the tropical jungle. I was awed by the lush landscape of primary rainforest that stretched as far as the eye could see. When we returned the following year, I was shocked to discover mile after mile of barren land. Everything was gone. My heart mourned for the beauty and wildlife that was lost. Right then and there, I committed to do something. I was 10 years old and was prepared to 'save the world'! That formative moment led me to pursue my studies and career in Environmental Management.

I got my first job in 2010 as a climate change researcher on a United Nations Environment Project (UNEP). It involved working with agricultural institutes in various countries, as well as hearing first-hand from farmers and practitioners in China, Kenya, and Niger on how unpredictable the growing seasons had been. A Kenyan farmer invited us to stomp our feet on his land to experience the extent to which it had dried up and hardened, causing his crops to fail. The rains were too late in Kenya, while Niger's severe drought led to a famine that left 7.3 million people in desperate need of food. Since then, what was predicted have now become common realities, with the world experiencing an increased intensity and frequency of extreme weather, from record-breaking temperatures every year to stronger hurricanes.

Christ, Community or Convenience?

I had known about the science of climate change and its devastating impacts since I was a child. But it was not until my early 20s in 2009 when the Lord's saving grace changed my life that I grew to discover who He is. I began to see that He not only desired to save my life, but to redeem all creation—animals and plants included! True hope entered my life and work, knowing that all creation is included within the scope of His saving and reconciling work on the cross.

In 2014, I attended the Lausanne Creation Care Network's Southeast Asian Regional Conference on Creation Care and the Gospel in the Philippines. It was four months after Typhoon Haiyan devastated parts of the country. The participants were pastors, practitioners, economists, biologists from Cambodia, Malaysia, Myanmar, Thailand, and more—all worshipping the same God. A missionary shared how she experienced the increased frequency and intensity of typhoons over the past 30 years in the country she served in. Once, she even had to hang on to her roof so that it did not fly off! Throughout the conference, I heard many such stories. I sat uncomfortably beside my brothers and sisters in Christ from neighbouring countries who were facing these impacts of climate change, knowing full well that my convenience and comfort in Singapore had contributed to their suffering. The comforts of air-conditioning, choosing cheaper options of products that did not have labels to demonstrate environmental track record, excessive food ordering and wastage—all contributed to my carbon footprint at the expense of others.

Creation Care Singapore Network

Following these encounters, a group of us from Singapore were convicted of the need to engage churches in Singapore and encourage them to address the crisis in creation from a biblical perspective. From that, Creation Care Singapore (CCSG) was birthed as a network of Christians in Singapore caring for God's creation as His image-bearers. We have organised creation care workshops, Christian and interfaith nature walks, and several rounds of our Creation Care Bible Study series that I developed under the guidance of David Gould (OMF's International Facilitator for Creation Care). The Creation Care Bible Study brought together young and old from different walks of life; who wanted to hear from God and encourage one another in awakening Christians to God's call as custodians of His creation.

In December 2015, the Lausanne Creation Care Network, in partnership with other Christian organisations, including A Rocha, Tearfund and the World Evangelical Alliance, were part of a contingent participating at COP21[1] in Paris to raise an evangelical voice on the issue of climate change and creation care as an outworking of our faith. COP21 was a critical moment in which climate change issues were brought to the forefront attention of the global Church. In God's wonderful provision, my church, Adam Road Presbyterian Church, supported me both financially and in prayer, to be sent as a CCSG representative to join the Lausanne delegation. We had several opportunities to proclaim God's name through prayer, music, and interfaith sharing sessions at the COP21 public zone.

---

1 Ed Brown, "Climate Change after Paris," *Lausanne Movement*, May 18, 2016, https://www.lausanne.org/content/lga/2016-05/climate-change-after-paris. See also "Climate News from Paris: A Rocha International," *A Rocha International*, accessed Oct. 31, 2019, https://www.arocha.org/en/raise-a-voice-for-the-climate/.

Leaders of various faiths came together to advocate for a deeper response to the climate crisis. One leader's declaration will stay etched in my mind, "We need to find a new paradigm of *being*, we need to *be* in a way that is not obsessed with accumulating stuff." Together, we recognised that the ecological crisis in all its complexity requires also a moral and spiritual response.

Called to a Ministry of Reconciliation

In reflecting on these various experiences and encounters, I am struck by how the two seemingly separate worlds of my professional development and personal faith are being woven together. As I plough through Scripture, I am constantly amazed at how much God has to say about caring for His creation! I see how God's purpose is unchanging—He is redeeming and reconciling His whole creation to Himself. Not only that, we are called to participate in this ministry of reconciliation: Christ's gift to us. With that unfolding truth in my life, my profession has become part of my ministry.

In my current role, part of my work involves developing my company's sustainability reporting. In many ways, sustainability reporting is my attempt at working towards God's model of restoration in Leviticus—Sabbath rest for the people, land, and animals, as well as the Jubilee. These laws enacted the great reset where debts were forgiven, property restored, and slaves freed to their families. They ensured that God's people lived in ways that reflected good relationships with God, one another, and the rest of creation. In living according to God's will for His whole creation, *all* can flourish, sustained by His grace and love.

While God's call to me since 1994 remains unchanged, it has deepened the core of who I am in relation to my calling and the One who calls me. He is my Rock amidst changing circumstances. This has built my confidence in Him. He is the present and ultimate Hope for me as well as for all creation, as He continues to reconcile all things to Himself, things in heaven or on earth, by making peace through His blood shed on the cross.

Caring for God's creation is not a "green movement", it is a prophetic response to our ecological crisis:

> …our ministry of reconciliation is a matter of great joy and hope and we would care for creation even if it were not in crisis. We are faced with a crisis that is pressing, urgent… We can no longer afford complacency and endless debate. Love for God, our neighbours, and the wider creation, as well as our passion for justice, compel us to "urgent and prophetic ecological responsibility"[2]

---

[2] "Creation Care and the Gospel: Jamaica Call to Action," *Lausanne Movement*, accessed Jan. 19, 2018, https://www.lausanne.org/content/statement/creation-care-call-to-action.

Resources

1. *Climate change summary of impacts in Singapore. Environmental issues threaten our survival.*[3]

   - 13 out of the past 15 years have been the warmest in Singapore's historical record since 1929.[4]
   - 50% of Singapore's water is currently sourced from Linggiu reservoir in Johor where water levels have been decreasing to a record low of 20% in 2016.[5]
   - Given that we import over 90% of our food, Singapore is vulnerable to increasing food prices.[6] Thus, any shift in global food supply places our food security at risk.

2. *Some measures taken in Singapore*

   - Singapore's carbon tax (first payment in 2020, based on emissions in 2019) will be enacted on large direct emitters to incentivise emissions reduction.

---

3 "Impact of Climate Change on Singapore," *National Climate Change Secretariat*, accessed Oct. 31, 2019, https://www.nccs.gov.sg/climate-change-and-singapore/national-circumstances/impact-of-climate-change-on-singapore.

4 Winston Chow, "How Vulnerable Is Singapore to Climate Change?" *Straits Times*, Sept. 7, 2018, https://www.straitstimes.com/singapore/how-vulnerable-is-spore-to-climate-change.

5 "'Significant Risk' Linggiu Reservoir May Dry out This Year: Vivian Balakrishnan," *CNA*, Mar. 31, 2017, https://www.channelnewsasia.com/news/singapore/significant-risk-linggiu-reservoir-may-dry-out-this-year-vivian--7555154.

6 Siau Ming En, "The Big Read: Far from people's minds, but food security a looming issue," *Today Singapore*, May 26, 2017, https://www.todayonline.com/singapore/big-read-far-peoples-minds-food-security-looming-issue.

God Unchanging in a Changing Climate

- Sustainability reporting is mandatory for all SGX-listed companies. This requires organisations to be accountable of how they manage economic, environmental, social, and governance issues.

3. *A Christian response to climate change*
    - Our Christian distinctive in caring for creation: https://www.arocha.org/en/distinctives/.
    - Get connected with fellow Christians in creation care: http://lwccn.com/.
    - Lausanne Global Consultation on Creation Care and the Gospel—Call to Action: https://www.lausanne.org/content/statement/creation-care-call-to-action and https://www.lausanne.org/content/creation-care-an-infographic.
    - Creation Care Singapore Bible Study: https://tinyurl.com/creationcaresgstudy.

4. *Take action!*
    - Reduce plastic disposables used in the church and reduce number of paper bulletins.
    - Offset your carbon footprint: climatestewards.org.
    - Take a walk in nature with your community to enjoy God's beautiful creation!

Event Stewardship

Shoni Duesling

Shoni grew up in a small Canadian town called Waterford where she was surrounded by lakes, open fields, and a loving community. Her love for people led her to study Communications and later, a Masters in Theological Studies at Regent College. Shoni now lives in Singapore with her husband Lean Sing, where they live out their passion for creation care at work, church and home. Through her work at Biblical Graduate School of Theology (BGST) and elsewhere, Shoni welcomes every opportunity to help those around her flourish.

> 10kg of papers and folders.
>
> 300 plastic water bottles.
>
> 150 disposable coffee cups and stir sticks.
>
> 300 individual packets of cream and sugar.

This was the projected amount of waste that BGST's Inaugural Creation Care Conference, *God's Purpose for His World: Christians, Creation and the Renewal of All Things* could have generated. It would have been ironic, and perhaps even a tad hypocritical, that a conference purporting to teach about creation care would generate such an enormous amount of waste. But, thankfully, this was not the case! The BGST Creation Care Conference not only taught the biblical perspective of creation care, but it also provided an event planning model that facilitated a creation-friendly, sustainable event.

Keynote speaker Professor Rikk Watts highlighted the Christian's call to be God's hands and feet in relation to *ALL* of creation, not just humans. While we leave other sections of this book to discuss creation care theology, we look at how we attempted to be God's hands and feet through our event. We share our Stewardship Strategy, four key lessons we learned, and three steps for planning a well-stewarded event, all in hope that it will encourage you to embark on your own stewardship adventure.

1. Stewardship Strategy

In preparation for the conference, we brainstormed tangible ways to reinforce the message of creation care and sustainability. We decided to focus on revamping two most utilised processes at events: how we did our catering and the way we used our paper.

Catering and Water Bottles

We all know that food, plastic water bottle, and disposable dishware waste is far too common and excessive at catered events. Thus, we took the following steps to limit this wastage at the conference:

First, we encouraged participants to bring their own reusable bottles and refill them throughout the day. This did away with the need for single use plastic bottles. We also had the caterer create an additional water point for us by providing a cooler of water. To our delight, many people brought their own reusable bottles!

Second, we used reusable dishware instead of disposables. We rented glassware for tea breaks and encouraged participants to bring their own cutlery and reusable containers for lunch. Again, almost all brought their own cutlery and reusable containers, making the lunch scene a mural speckled with dishes of all colours, shapes and sizes. This was an encouraging sight, to say the least.

Third, we set up a clearing station for tea breaks so that participants were able to put dishes and waste into the appropriate bin or bag. This station eliminated the need for a catering staff to help us clean up after ourselves.

Fourth, we had Elsie's Kitchen cater food that was sourced as locally as possible—mainly from Singapore and Malaysia

—thus reducing the event's carbon footprint. We also replaced individual packets of sugar and creamer with bowls of each in bulk.

Paper
Paper materials can be helpful tools, but are hardcopies absolutely necessary? The answer for us was no.

For our conference, digital handouts were viable replacements for printed ones. By going digital, we saved time and money and were able to send a broader range of content—videos, coupons and links—to participants in digital folders. We also digitised our Q&A, shifting from paper slips to an interactive online Q&A platform.

2. Insightful Lessons

Lesson #1: Worship
Event planning can be a form of worship! It is an opportunity to create meaningful, life-giving experiences by working closely with God and other people. We worship him by being mindful that stewarding resources well is a way of acknowledging him as the provider, and that respecting what he has created is a way to show respect for him.

Lesson #2: Prayer
We cannot emphasise enough the power of prayer! Communing and communicating with God meant that we could work with our hands while trusting God to enact his plan. To our delight, the event ran smoother than we could have imagined. The largest shock was that 95% of people brought their own dishes!

Lesson #3: Plan, Pre-empt, Provide

It is crucial to Plan, Pre-empt and Provide. For example, we learnt that washing points were not feasible at our conference. Hence, we: (1) *planned* around this by asking participants to bring *lidded containers* that they could close up and take home to wash; (2) *pre-empted* participants through reminder emails, communicating that dishes would need to be taken home to be washed; and (3) *provided* recycled-newspaper for participants to clean or wrap their dishes with. The result of Planning, Pre-empting, and Providing was that participants were extremely happy to take part in our creation care initiatives!

Lesson #4: Change Starts with Awareness

Creation care is an extremely new topic for many Christians, so you may be met with resistance when you broach the topic with fellow believers or church leaders. In these times, remember that any form of change must start with awareness. Sustainable living will happen when people have an awareness of how creation care aligns with their personal faith, and understand how they can apply creation care in clear and tangible steps.

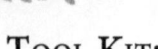

TOOL KIT:
THREE STEPS FOR PLANNING A WELL-STEWARDED EVENT

1. Cater Sustainably →**Food**: Buy Local, Buy Less; **Dishware**: BYO or Rent Reusables
2. Paper → **Digitise** what you can (materials, registration, etc.) and when you really need to print something, use Forest Stewardship Council (FSC) Certified paper
3. Plastic Water Bottles → Encourage people to bring reusable water bottles

While these lessons and steps are certainly not exhaustive, they are "low hanging fruit" to get us started. With over one million Christians in Singapore enjoying regular communal gatherings involving food, the opportunity for impact is tremendous. So, let us work together, starting with small but active steps and doing our part to make a difference. Let us cover our initiatives in prayer, not be afraid of making mistakes, and remember: most people are willing to make small changes to care for creation; they just need us to explain the *why* and *how*.

You can download or stream *God's Purpose for His World: Christians, Creation and the Renewal of All Things* at http://bit.ly/BGSTCreationCare.

Cornelius Plantinga Jr. offers this definition of *shalom*:

"The webbing together of God, humans, and all creation in justice, fulfillment, and delight is what the Hebrew prophets called shalom. We call it 'peace,' but it means far more than just peace of mind or cease-fire between enemies…[it] means universal flourishing, wholeness, and delight—a rich state of affairs in which natural needs are satisfied and natural gifts fruitfully employed, all under the arch of God's love. *Shalom*, in other words, is the way things are supposed to be."[1]

Where do we see shalom *disrupted in creation? How can we manifest God's* shalom *as the living, breathing body of Christ?*

---

1 Cornelius Plantinga Jr., *Engaging in God's World: A Christian Vision of Faith, Learning, and Living* (Grand Rapids, MI: William B. Eerdmans, 2002).

Sayang Kalimantan

Wally Tham

Wally's storytelling career began in television and later moved into creating content and video campaigns for online platforms, which has won him international awards. Today, Wally's work in narrative includes organisational development for institutions and public interventions. Addressing issues of scarcity, identity, and innovation, Wally helps companies look at the stories that make us stronger. Through his ground-up group Stand Up for Our Singapore, he creates opportunities for the public to imagine the Singapore they could be proud of.

The following story has been captured in his award-winning documentary, Sayang Kalimantan.[1]

---

[1] *Sayang Kalimantan* was awarded Honorable Mention at the Sony Pictures *Picture This Festival 2018*. You can watch it here: https://vimeo.com/273320769.

There's No Smoke Without Fire

For a few days every year between May and September, Singapore becomes keenly aware of the peatland and forest fires raging in Kalimantan, Indonesia. The black smoke blows over and we become personally affected. The young, the elderly, and those with asthma are especially vulnerable to the onset of red eyes, runny noses, coughs, and increased risks of cardiac arrests.

But once the haze dissipates, we forget about it.

Unfortunately, this is not a problem that we can easily dismiss. The burning of these forests is closely linked with Singapore's consumption of palm oil, one of the most widely used vegetable oils in Southeast Asia. To meet the increasing demand for palm oil—which is used in our hawker food, chocolate, biscuits, cosmetics, soaps, and even our *teh si* and 3-in-1 instant coffee—palm oil plantations have resorted to using the quickest and cheapest way to clear the land. With the rapid expansion of the palm oil sector, these plantations have now become the leading cause of these annual forest fires. They significantly contribute to the rise of greenhouse gas emissions, biodiversity loss, and indictments for human rights violations of local communities.[2]

---

[2] Per Liljas, "Indonesia: Fewer Forest Fires in 2016, but No Real Progress," *Time*, Dec. 13, 2016, https://time.com/4562009/indonesia-haze-forest-fires-palm-oil-deforestation/. Also Alice Cuddy, "How Local Elites Earn Money from Burning Land in Indonesia." *Mongabay Environmental News*, Feb. 2, 2017, https://news.mongabay.com/2017/01/how-local-elites-earn-money-from-burning-land-in-indonesia/.

So why should we care about the haze in Kalimantan—a story of people far away who are suffering, who seem to be responsible for our suffering too? The high demand for palm oil in countries like Singapore makes the forest fires a frightening reality that is unlikely to disappear on its own. The interconnectedness of the world today makes it just as much our responsibility to do something about this issue as it is the Indonesians.

A Burning Fear

My first trip to Kalimantan was a social initiative to distribute N95 masks. I also conducted workshops to educate the locals on how to use these masks. In the midst of all this, I could not help but wonder, "Is giving out one mask in such a severe situation really going to help?"

The gravity of the issue hit me hard during a particular incident on that trip. I had stayed behind to run a few extra workshops. Little did I know that the airport would close indefinitely on the day I planned to leave. Trapped in a hotel room without any air filters, I became anxious as days went by. Eventually, my anxiety culminated in a panic attack. I could not breathe; I was so overwhelmed. I thought I was going to die because I was never getting out of there. It was completely irrational, but so very real at the time.

This experience brought me closer to the daily realities and struggles of my friends in Kalimantan. If this was the kind of terror that could strike in a single instance, I could only imagine how intense three months of fear would be for them.

Here are some numbers to put it into perspective. In Singapore, the PSI levels of the 2015 haze were between 300–400. The highest in Beijing, known for her air pollution, is at a catastrophic 800–1000. But in Kalimantan, the highest recorded level then was 2900!

The Kalimantan Project

Challenged by my experience, I spent the next two years working on a sustainable solution. Eventually the team at my company, Big Red Button, and I designed a haze shelter. It was a tightly sealed concrete space with a two-stage filtration system, providing clean air day and night.

Soon after, UNICEF approached us and asked if we could create a solution for rural villages near the forest. I was initially frustrated with the task of solving yet another problem. But God started to shift my perspective. I started to see my commitment to this project as an act of love, an expression of how I can "love my neighbour as myself" (Mark 12:31). While trapped in that room in Kalimantan, all I wanted was to be protected from the haze. If I loved my neighbours as I loved myself, I would want to protect them too.

I am not an engineer, just a "video guy". But after two weeks of praying, God gave me the idea of a dome shelter constructed from rattan and bamboo. It would make a clean-air space to sleep in and, since it is made from freely available or affordable materials, easy enough to replicate in a rural village. We only needed funding for the fan filters. We named this second prototype, "Sarang Kecil" (Little Nest).

I was amazed at what God could do through us: we went from having zero viable clean-air spaces to two prototypes!

Next Steps for the Kalimantan Project

People keep labelling me and this work as "environmental". But in truth, it was adaptation work—a Band-Aid that does not address the root cause of the forest fires in Kalimantan. That is why our latest effort of planting trees is more proactive in mitigating habitat loss. Through our partners, we plant tree saplings and aim to nurture them for 15–20 years. The saplings will capture carbon as they grow. Once they reach maturity, they can be harvested, sold, and the money will help fund the next batch of trees.

Since starting in mid 2018, we have planted about 1500 trees. Capturing about 40 kg of carbon per tree every year till they mature, these trees will absorb and store an estimated 60,000 kg of carbon annually for the next 15 years. This is the work that is actively restoring the land. This is the pivot we hope to scale. If we can get the right partners on board, companies or individuals can be planting many more trees.

Through this project, I am becoming more and more conscious of how connected I am to everything and everyone. In his wisdom, God has designed creation as one integrated web of relationships; all of life is ecologically interdependent. Whether it is Kalimantan or elsewhere on the earth, we are all inextricably linked. And because we are connected, I care deeply about people and places. In caring, my frustration of being in Singapore and feeling hopeless is gradually resolving. Certainly, there were many points at which I felt like throwing in the towel. While I had friends who prayed with and encouraged me, I often felt alone. At times, I was exhausted and even really broke, but these feelings would come and go. Nonetheless, my conviction in this mission has never wavered. We can mend our world with love and action. Hopefully, the more we tell this story, the more we can invite others to do the same. Everyone can be a part of something, even in a far-off place like Kalimantan.

ONLY ONE EARTH

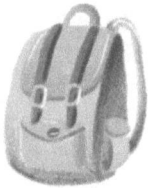

Khee Shihui

Shihui started speaking up about environmental issues after seeing the devastating impact of trash choking marine life in oceans. Outside of work in the social innovation sector, she shares about Bring Your Own (BYO) and low-waste practices on her Instagram account @tabaogirl, to show that it's possible to make a difference in our daily lives. Every effort can be a prayer and an act of devotion to God. She believes wonderment can be found by appreciating and protecting God's big and little creatures.

"Saint Francis, faithful to Scripture, invites us to see nature as a magnificent book in which God speaks to us and grants us a glimpse of his infinite beauty and goodness. 'Through the greatness and the beauty of creatures one comes to know by analogy their maker' (Wisdom 13:5); indeed, 'his eternal power and divinity have been made known through his works since the creation of the world' (Romans 1:20)"[1] ~Pope Francis

On the morning of 29 May 2017, I woke up to a shocking discovery: "The Great Barrier Reef is damaged beyond repair and can no longer be saved, say scientists."[2] Beneath this news headline was a photo of bleached corals. Where were the colourful anemones hosting the darting clownfish made famous by *Finding Nemo*? The reef depicted was utterly lifeless. As a diver, all I could think about was "How did human beings destroy what had flourished for millennia…in mere decades?"

A deep grief welled up, then, anger: at countries that generated the largest greenhouse emissions; at the frantic pace of urbanisation and industrialisation; at corporations responsible for deforestation; overfishing; unabated mining and drilling; at car manufacturers; fast-fashion; the industrial

---

1 "Encyclical Letter Laudato Si' of the Holy Father Francis on Care for Our Common Home," Paragraph 12, *Vatican*, accessed Nov. 14, 2019, http://w2.vatican.va/content/francesco/en/encyclicals/documents/papa-francesco_20150524_enciclica-laudato-si.html.

2 Helena Horton, "Great Barrier Reef is damaged beyond repair and can no longer be saved, say scientists," *Telegraph*, May 29, 2019, https://www.telegraph.co.uk/news/2017/05/29/great-barrier-reef-damaged-beyond-repair-can-no-longer-saved/.

food system and unsustainable agriculture; then at society, for not caring for our one and only home: Earth.

Finally, I was upset with myself, having unquestioningly lived a life of modern comforts and conveniences. I had never once stopped to consider who or what paid the true cost of my lifestyle and choices—choices that seemed to be fixed options presented to us by governments and corporations that make the decisions upstream.

***

> "Hope has two beautiful daughters. Their names are anger and courage; anger at the way things are, and courage to see that they do not remain the way they are." ~St Augustine of Hippo

The following day, something had irreversibly changed for me. If nature is how God gives us an infinitesimal glimpse of His beauty and goodness, what then is the responsibility of us as God's children, to protect and care for His creation?

While I could not impact policies or global business practices directly, I could take control of my choices. I could share with others about the connections between climate change, environmental degradation, and consumerism.

Initially, I had no plan. I started by bringing reusable utensils to work. Subsequently, a lunchbox and takeaway cup. Then, a tote-bag and produce bag. I brought along what I needed from home and refrained from buying new items for my zero-waste lifestyle. I began posting photos on

Facebook to share my daily efforts. Colleagues and friends started noticing these changes.

One day, a friend suggested I use Instagram to raise eco-awareness. That was the birth of @tabaogirl! I soon started engaging people beyond my immediate social networks. A few months into my @tabaogirl journey, an acquaintance remarked, "One person won't make much difference lah. This habit is inconvenient for those around you!" As an engineer, I was trained to make decisions based on rigorous evidence. By downloading a tally app to keep track of the disposables I avoided by bringing my own items, I could show the impact of committed individual action!

Whenever strangers in an event buffet line were curious about my tabao box or people in a cafe asked about my BYO cup, I would chat with them and show my tabao tally. This tended to lead to more questions after: "How do you wash your box? Isn't it troublesome?" "What happens if you are meeting four other friends?" "Aren't you wasting water because you need to wash the items?" Answering these FAQs patiently was often the nudge someone needed to BYO! (See my cheat sheet at the end for the responses I use.)

At other times, the comments were less kind. "You're slowing down the line, hurry." "Why change if others don't?" "Don't eat, don't buy anything, don't live lor! Then you won't use anything!" I decided to use these comments as learning points. I prepared the exact payment for hawkers and observed which stalls I would disrupt the least with my BYO request.

At times, my BYO requests generated conversations. Hawkers revealed their difficulty in finding stall assistants, forcing them to use disposables, even for dine-in customers. Stall owners in the CBD talked about escalating rent and shrinking outlet sizes, so washing utensils and crockery were not as feasible. Wait staff shared about outbursts from impatient office workers, which led to food being pre-packed in disposables to speed up transactions.

Each conversation showed the intricacies of how urban living changed the way we interacted with one another and with nature. Each experience revealed reasons people had for preferring the status quo, even if they knew it was not ideal. These encounters helped me shape more compassionate ways to reach out.

As I faithfully documented my actions in 2018, my waste reduction journey moved from obligation to devotion. I reconnected with old friends and made new ones because of our shared love for God's creation and mutual encouragement. My eco journey, with its failures and limitations, deepened my faith and relationship with God. Being a recovering perfectionist and an adult convert to Roman Catholicism, it took me some time to realise that it is not about more reducing, reusing, recycling—or the reinforcing of more rules. Instead, the commitment to live out the principles of creation care matters much more than getting it "perfect".

The challenges I face on this eco-journey keep me close to God at every turn: be it the struggle to empathise with those who are still finding the motivation to lead a more sustainable lifestyle, or channelling my criticism into gentler words of outreach, or even prayers for the people, businesses, and organisations that have yet to see how their actions negatively impact the environment. The conviction to this new way of living is hopefully a testimony to His Spirit moving in my life.

By the end of 2018, after tracking my efforts for 365 days, I had avoided 438 plastic bags, 420 disposable utensils, 303 throwaway cups, 246 plastic straws, 108 takeaway boxes, and 69 disposable bowls and plates. That may sound insignificant given the massive global challenge of overconsumption of plastics—but imagine all of Singapore, or even the world, making a similar effort!

Climate scientists report that the world has only 12 years left to avert catastrophic global warming.[3] When more eco-conscious consumers and citizens vote with their dollars and actions, we are signalling to corporations and governments that changes in business and legislative practices need to happen urgently! Amidst the increasing awareness and scientific know-how of our generation in caring for this earth, it is my hope that the Church will arise to take her place in participating in God's work of renewing His creation.

What will our response as God's people be?

---

3 "Global Warming of 1.5°C," *IPCC*, accessed Oct. 31, 2019, https://www.ipcc.ch/sr15/.

My Cheat Sheet:

1. How do you wash your box after each meal, isn't it troublesome?

At many eating places, there is usually a sink with a soap dispenser conveniently located. If not, I'll wash my items at the public toilet.

2. What happens if you are meeting four other friends?

I once brought 10 plates and 10 sets of cutlery to a gathering! These days, I'd ask my friends if they need me to pack utensils for them, and that prompt will usually lead to them bringing their own utensils too.

3. Aren't you wasting more water because you need to wash the items?

Plastic/paper disposables also require electricity, water, raw materials, and fossil fuels in their production and transport. Bringing and washing our utensils uses less resources overall. However, it is really about being mindful of the lifecycle of every item that we buy and use. For example, if I buy a metal straw but only use it once or twice, then it would have been far better to use a plastic straw, since that took much lesser resources to make. If I bought a new cotton tote bag, I would have to use it at least 127 times to offset the resources it took to make, against the use of a plastic bag. In this case, it might be more environmentally friendly to re-use a plastic bag four or five times, rather than buying a new cotton bag.

4. Do I need to buy anything to kick-start my BYO journey?

It would be really helpful to look for items already available in your home, such as an existing water bottle, or lunchbox, or even a set of utensils. Try out the BYO habit for a few days, and if you find it achievable, you can continue to use these items from home, without incurring more costs, or buying items that you don't really need—inadvertently causing more wastage!

5. If I am not ready to BYO, what are steps I can take to be more environmentally friendly?

If you look at your everyday habits or consumption, perhaps you can start with refusing what you don't need, such as goody bags or freebies; or reducing the amounts of food, items or clothing you buy to reduce wastage, reusing what you have; and lastly, recycling what is still possible to recycle!

6. Where do I go to find a community of people to encourage me?

You may want to join the "Journey to Zero Waste Life in Singapore" Facebook group. There are many like-minded people who are passionate about the environment there and they trade tips and tricks on staying green. Alternatively, you can consider following zero waste Instagram accounts, simply search hashtags like "#zerowastesg", "#byosingapore" and pick your favourite accounts to follow!

St Francis of Assisi was a Catholic friar most well-known for his patronage of animals and the natural world. He loved God so greatly that he had an affectionate kinship with the created community[1] of his Father. This reverence and love was characteristic of his ministry and his life.

We invite you, as channels of God's shalom for his creation, to make this prayer, attributed to St Francis, yours:

> Lord, make me an instrument of your peace.
> Where there is hatred, let me sow love.
> Where there is injury, pardon.
> Where there is doubt, faith.

---

[1] Most well-known is *Canticle of Brother Sun and Sister Moon of St Francis of Assisi*.

Where there is despair, hope.
Where there is darkness, light.
Where there is sadness, joy.
O Divine Master,
Grant that I may not so much seek to be consoled, as to console;
To be understood, as to understand;
To be loved, as to love.
For it is in giving that we receive.
It is in pardoning that we are pardoned,
And it is in dying that we are born to Eternal Life.
Amen.

Trusting in the Gardener's Pruning

Shirene Chen & Ken Yeong

Ten years ago, Shirene and Ken took their first steps to change their careers from corporate work to creation care.

Shirene has been an urban food gardener and teacher for the past seven years. She runs food gardening workshops and coaches families and organisations on edible gardens through her company, Diglings. She sees the garden as a window to the larger world and loves to connect food gardening to all of life—whether as a source of nutrition and medicine, an education in environmental science, an artistic expression, a therapy for the body and soul, a community-building project, or a play space for grown-ups and children.

Ken has worked in conservation with WWF and corporate sustainability with Earthworm Foundation for the past seven years. He draws from these experiences as well as his hands-on gardening with his wife, Shirene—in their food garden in Kuala Lumpur—to create imaginative, experiential and multi-disciplinary nature education programmes for families and organisations. Ken loves teaching and sharing the joy and wonder he discovers in nature.

Together with their son, River, they are finding their voice and place in this work in God's kingdom.

Before we fell in love with each other, we were in love with the great outdoors. We loved climbing crags and diving wrecks, long journeys to wild places, and the rush of outdoor adventure sports. We did not know it at the time, but on our lonely, separate journeys to conquer mountains and oceans, we were really searching for solace and significance. The vastness of nature made us feel that we were a part of something larger than ourselves; we devoured nature to fill the void inside.

When we met, we thought we had found our soulmate. However, after we got married, we found ourselves fighting for more and more from each other, and that devoured our marriage. It turned out that soulmates could also kill each other.

Somewhere between the devouring of nature and the devouring of marriage, we became Christians. It was at this time that our relationship with nature grew beyond recreation and consumption to include concern for its degradation. While volunteering with an environmental organisation, I attended a permaculture course. I came home crying to Ken, "The planet is dying! What are we going to do about it?! Why are the Christians not doing anything?!" I had not met a single Christian during my time with the environmental organisation or at the permaculture course. This was ten years ago.

Following that cry of despair, a cascade of events gave us courage and conviction to change our careers from corporate work to creation care. We met Mel and Dan, who introduced us to A Rocha's work and values. We spent days animatedly talking about this kind of work and life. We listened to sermons by Pastor Wong Fong Yang and Pastor Tan Soo-Inn on living out our faith from Monday to Friday in the marketplace and our hearts quickened. Pastor Wong then helped Ken to obtain a scholarship from the Council for World Mission to study a Master in Environment. Six years ago, we completed our environmental studies in Australia and returned to Malaysia to work.

We began our career change carrying an important and bold mission to have a profound impact on people and planet through work in creation care. But, unbeknownst to us, we also held an underlying belief that following our vocational calling, marrying our soulmates, and raising our child to love nature would automatically lead to well-paying, satisfying jobs, a euphoric marriage, and a nature-basking, bug-hunting child. We were to discover that real life, like ecosystems, does not operate in linearity.

Today, Ken works with businesses to improve their environmental and social impact. But corporate sustainability was not his first choice of work. He had started in his dream job in traditional conservation that dealt directly with biodiversity and ecosystem restoration. However, he soon realised that it could not pay enough to cover our family's finances. He had to give that up to work in new conservation with businesses to support our family financially.

As for me, I wanted to do a home business so that I could be at home to raise our son. Before I dug my first shovelful of dirt, I had one of those dreamy-soft focus visions of myself contentedly tending our cottage garden while showing my young child the wonders of creation, all the while making a small but sufficient income from my gardening venture. I soon discovered thorns and thistles bristling in my patch of Eden. Clay that turned to mud when wet but rock solid when dry meant backbreaking toil in the soil. As for wondrous explorations in nature with our son, while we do spend time gardening and hiking together, he prefers football and Lego.

Gradually, over the ten years of our journey, all kinds of pests and tests in our marriage, parenting, garden, and Ken's work shrunk our ambitions immensely. These disappointments naturally pierced our bubble of entitlement. Both the scale of the home garden and the industry that Ken works in showed us how difficult and seemingly hopeless it is to make any profound impact on the world at large. We realised our search for solace and significance could not be satisfied in nature or even in *caring* for nature.

Instead, solace and significance can only be found in the One who is bigger than nature. Our shattered expectations enlarged our need for God alone to redeem our love for nature, our work, marriage, and parenting for his purposes. And we understand that humans are meant to be a blessing to creation because we are made in the image of God who created and continues to sustain everything on earth. We also experience that as we cultivate our garden, the garden in turn cultivates us. God may be more interested in the fruits of our inner garden that grow even as we coax fruits from the garden of our home. Indeed, by his blessings, we have enjoyed more and sweeter fruits in our marriage, family, and garden.

And so we carry on.

We take heart from the words of Eugene Peterson:

> There's a great temptation in making a conclusion to a story to make things tidy. When theological and moral issues are involved, the temptation is especially strong. But tidiness does violence to both Scripture and life [...] The David story is full of odd angles, unexplained mysteries, awkward moments, and the conclusion honors the persistent presence of God in all of this. Insofar as this is also the story of every man and woman, we see ourselves affirmed in our basic humanness, confronted with the inescapable conditions of our culture, and from time to time finding out true voice at the center, speaking to God and for God.[1]

It is our deep prayer that these words of our messy, weedy story are part of "finding our true voice at the center, speaking to God and for God".

---

[1] Eugene Peterson, *The Message 100 Devotional Bible: The Story of God in Sequence* (Colorado Springs, CO: NavPress, 2015), 470.

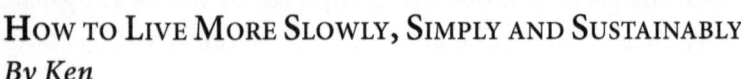

How to Live More Slowly, Simply and Sustainably
By Ken

We live in time—a gift of creation—but believe we have so little of it to live well. Safeguard time for reflecting, praying slowly, daydreaming, and just zoning out (not being distracted by the phone!). Our mind and spirit need the free space to explore life-giving things. Ideas will come, questions will arise, realisation will set in, with time.

There is dignity in chores, and doing them regularly has the grace of reminding us of a simple life. When we lead simpler lives, it tends to be more sustainable.

Celebrate the simple wonders of creation in everyday life. Get up before dawn to immerse yourself in the cool fresh air. Savour the special flavour of a cempedak. Admire patterns of nature, like the many shapes of leaves. Who knows, appreciation may lead to action...

A traveller on a bicycle sees, hears, smells, feels, and experiences much more than another on a train. Do we want to speed through life and collect many still photos, or do we want to slow down and be blessed with the privilege of being a part of the living moment?

We consume things. Companies sell things to us. Suppose we tell these companies, produce sustainably, or we won't buy. Harness your power as consumers by opting for sustainability. Companies are beginning to listen. Really.

Every creature has an impact on their environment and other creatures. Yet, a biodiverse (crowded!) nature works because it follows God's command, "Be fruitful" (Genesis 1), and Jesus' advice, "It is more blessed to give than to receive" (Acts 20:35). Do likewise. Sustainable consumption is a particularly powerful way to give because it sometimes requires paying a higher but also fairer price, and it requires giving your time to do some research on the companies, and engaging with them.

Sustainability is, by nature, a public issue. Armchair activism works at times, but getting out and reaching out to your community works better because people connect better when together. When people get together, they start to draw attention to themselves and policymakers will then take notice. When personal activism combines with good policymaking, the chances of good sustainability outcomes are multiplied!

Sustainability has come to define the epoch we live in now. It is all encompassing because it affects everyone. It has become so big because we all contributed to the crisis. Therefore, our active participation will also help to lead to its resolution. It is no longer "what can one person do", but "how can I do something useful". Find your position in the domino effect.

Afterword

Quek Tze-Ming

Tze-Ming is the Director (Postgraduate Programmes) at the Biblical Graduate School of Theology (BGST), where he lectures in New Testament studies. Previously, he was a lawyer, and a campus ministry staff worker with the Fellowship of Evangelical Students. He has degrees from Regent College, Vancouver, and is a PhD candidate in New Testament Studies at the University of Cambridge. He is married to Sharon, and they have two daughters. In his spare time, he is a keen foodie, movie buff, and a patient Liverpool fan.

"We now understand God's rest to be at the same time the rest of his creation."[1] ~Dietrich Bonhoeffer

One of the distinctives Christians bring to the table of environmental concern is an eschatological horizon: where or on whom we base our hope. Unlike many environmental activists, Christians do not base our hope in humanity. This is not a crisis we have to solve by ourselves (even though we do have a big part and responsibility). Neither can we sort out this mess solely by our ingenuity in science, education, action, economics, or law and politics (though advances in these areas do help, as attested by the stories in this book). Ultimately, this is a spiritual issue, and our hope is in God. As Dave Bookless says:

> Yet, for Christians, the human heart cannot be changed by campaigns, collective action, or new consciousness. Only God's Spirit can re-order our disordered desires. And, whilst our short-term, proximate, hopes will be dashed time and time again, our ultimate hope is not in ourselves, but in God's saving work in Christ, through whose death on the cross all things in heaven and on earth will be reconciled to God.[2]

How does God's Spirit re-order our disordered desires? Through spiritual disciplines that develop habits of the heart. In the area of creation care, one spiritual discipline

---

[1] Dietrich Bonhoeffer, *Creation and Fall Temptation: Two Biblical Studies* (New York, NY: Simon & Schuster, 1997).

[2] Dave Bookless, "Greta goes to the UN," *A Rocha*, Sep. 25, 2019, https://www.arocha.org/en/news/greta-goes-to-the-un/.

that can help is that of Sabbath-keeping. In many ways, Sabbath-keeping *is* earth-keeping.[3]

First, Sabbath-keeping helps us **look around**. The creation account in Genesis 1 tells us that God did not just create humans, he created a whole ecosystem for human and non-human flourishing. Creation as an intricate system has Sabbath built into it. And, just as the human body suffers if it lacks appropriate and timely rest, all creation suffers if rest is taken out of its interconnected system. The naturalist John Muir once wrote about this interconnectedness, "When we try to pick out anything by itself, we find it hitched to everything else in the universe."[4] Once we see this, we can describe our current environmental crisis thus: Creation is not operating the way it was meant to (climate change, species loss), because humans have been abusing and misusing it as selfish consumers rather than caring stewards. We do not cease in our restless overconsumption and so creation gets no rest and is exhausted.

Practising Sabbath makes us follow God—when he rested on the seventh day—in delighting in what he has made. On the Sabbath we cease from using or exploiting non-human creation. Instead we immerse ourselves in, and cherish God's intricate, interconnected, good creation, of which we are a part, as stewards and carers.

---

[3] I am indebted to A.J. Swoboda's, *Subversive Sabbath: The Surprising Power of Rest in a Nonstop World* (Grand Rapids, MI: Brazos, 2018) for this catchphrase, and some of the following ideas.

[4] John Muir, *My First Summer in the Sierra* (Boston, MA: Houghton Mifflin, 1911), 110.

Secondly, Sabbath-keeping helps us to *look up*. And when we look up we see God, not our own image. The psalmist says, "The earth is the Lord's and the fullness thereof, the world and those who dwell therein..." (Psalm 24:1 ESV). Creation's Lord and Master is our God, and not us.

Practising Sabbath reminds us that the world gets on fine even when we cease from work, because God is the one who sustains it. We are reminded of our humanity—dependent like the rest of creation on God—as we hand authority back to the One to whom it truly and already belongs. We are also freed from the crushing burden of "saving the earth", even as we advocate for creation care, because our ultimate hope is not on human endeavour but on God's work.

Finally, Sabbath-keeping helps us to *look forward*. Sabbath is a picture of the final rest which is the culmination and fulfilment of God's saving work in Christ, in reconciling all things in heaven and on earth to himself (Hebrews 4; Colossians 1:20). We return to what was said earlier about the eschatological horizon. Paul makes the point that all creation has that forward look, indeed yearning for that Day when it "will be set free from its bondage to corruption and obtain the freedom of the glory of the children of God" (Romans 8:21 ESV).

Practising Sabbath is a foretaste for that final Day, when we, with all creation, will no longing be groaning, but rejoicing in the birth of the new heavens and new earth.

This book is about the ways Christians can *do more* in caring for creation, whether as part of organisations or businesses, in community or as individuals. It is curiously apt that we end with a reflection on how we all need to begin with Sabbath-keeping, the spiritual discipline of *doing less*.

Appendix

Location: Tampines Eco-Green
Date: 29th February 2016
Time: 7.30 p.m. – 9.00 p.m.

S/N	Time	Species	Weather	General Habitat	Remarks
1	7.50 pm	*Microhyla heymonsi (c)*	Windy	Dry grassy patch near pond	Chorus of frogs calling along stretch
2	8.10 pm	*Polypaedates leucomystax*	Windy	On the dry granite chips stony ground	
3	8.20 pm	*Kaloula pulchra*	Windy	On base of tree, near roots	
4	8.21 pm	*Kaloula pulchra*	Windy	On base of tree, near roots	
5	8.30 pm	*Michroyla heymonsi (c)*	Windy	Dry grassy patch	Chorus of frogs calling along stretch
6	8.35 pm	*Polypaedates leucomystax*	Windy	Dry grassy patch	Single solitary call
7	8.40 pm	*Polypaedates leucomystax*	Windy	On tree, near pond	

Legend
(c): calling individuals

Observations
- Observed a number of geckos.
- Observed a great number of night jars (at one time, 5 individuals on track ahead of us).
- Saw a juvenile swamp eel in shallow water-body (towards marshes platform). There was also an unidentified black fish (about 2 inches in size) here.
- Observed a number of goby fish in pond at entrance, also a couple of water hens!

About the Editors

*When **Melissa** first encountered A Rocha in 2003, it felt like coming home to family. AR's founders Peter and Miranda Harris invited Mel and her husband Daniel to join the international team to film their conservation work around the world. She left her work in television and served in A Rocha International for 13 years, supported by Zion Bishan BP Church as a missionary. In 2006, she and Dan lived and worked in community with AR Canada. Since returning in 2008, she's been connecting with kindred spirits, and raising awareness of creation care in Singapore. She and Prarthi facilitate Friends of A Rocha in Singapore and long to see Christians connect faith and ecology. Mel finds great joy in walking with people on their creation care journey. Today, she is a dog trainer and helps people and dogs heal through Natural Dog Training.*

***Prarthi** really loves amphibians and reptiles—she counts the Malayan Horned Frog as her favourite frog species ever! She spent most of her NUS life studying these and many other fascinating creatures and bio-systems. This was made all the richer through her time in the Varsity Christian Fellowship in seeing that caring for creation is something God is concerned with. Upon graduation, she joined the Fellowship of Evangelical Students in 2015, where she has been serving as a campus ministry staff-worker ever since. As Prarthi goes about life, she desires to seek right relationships while marvelling at God's beauty and wonder in creation, and invites others to do likewise.*

FRIENDS OF A ROCHA IN SINGAPORE

Formed in 2009, Friends of A Rocha in Singapore grew out of an informal community of volunteers and supporters of A Rocha. It continues to initiate a local expression of creation care that was inspired by A Rocha's mission and values: Christian, conservation, community, cross-cultural, and cooperation.

If you would like to know more, get involved, or get in touch with the contributors of this book, you can contact us at *sg.friends@arocha.org*.

GRACEWORKS

Graceworks is a publishing and training consultancy based in Singapore, dedicated to promoting spiritual friendship in church and society, and seeing lives transformed through books that present truth for life.

Our publications can be found on our online store, *www.graceworks.com.sg/store*. Paperbacks are also available on Book Depository and Amazon. eBooks on Kindle, iBooks and Kobo. You can contact us at *enquiries@graceworks.com.sg*, or follow us on Facebook (@GraceworksSG) and Instagram (graceworkssg).

www.ingramcontent.com/pod-product-compliance
Lightning Source LLC
LaVergne TN
LVHW041948070526
838199LV00051BA/2946